Justice in Jesus' Name

Early Black Apostolic Involvement in the Civil Rights Struggle

James I. Clark, Jr.

Seymour Press **SP**

Justice in Jesus' Name: Early Black Apostolic Involvement in Civil Rights Struggles

© James I. Clark, Jr. 2023

ISBN: 978-1-938373-68-8

LCCN: : 2023944114

© Seymour Press 2023
Lanham, MD

Unless otherwise noted, all scripture is from the King James Version of the Bible.

Table of Contents

Appreciation

Many people assisted in preparing this manuscript for publication, and I would like to acknowledge all of them. Dr. Michael O. West read the manuscript and strongly advised me to publish this work. Deacon Alexander Stewart impressed upon me, more times than I can count, that publishing my manuscript would be a blessing to the Church of Our Lord Jesus Christ of the Apostolic Faith (COOLJC). Thanks to my friends and brothers in Christ who enthusiastically endorsed the manuscript, inspiring me to press on to its publication, and thank you to Dr. Estrelda Alexander and the Seymour Press team, who agreed that *Justice in Jesus' Name* was ready for the public.

Dedication

To my family, especially my dear wife, who has supported me along every step in this journey. This work would not have been possible without them. And to my Christ Temple family for their continued prayerful support.

Preface

In 1990, as I completed candidacy for the Master of Divinity degree at the Union Theological Seminary in New York, I was discussing my topic with my mentor, the late Professor James Melvin Washington. I offered many unstructured thoughts as to a subject until Dr. Washington posed a question about the organization to which my church belongs—the Church of Our Lord Jesus Christ of the Apostolic Faith Inc. (COOLJC) and the tradition of which it is a part—Apostolic Pentecostalism. The question went something like, "Why not consider writing about your faith tradition?" Dr. Washington continued, "I know little about it, and it would be interesting to learn more."

The invitation to share my experience and understanding of my church and tradition set me on a trajectory on which I am still deeply engaged, and what a journey it has been. Undertaking this study expanded my awareness of the origins of the Church of Our Lord Jesus Christ and the history of the key events that have defined moments in the evolution of this great ministry. My research broadened and deepened my knowledge and appreciation of its establishmentarian, Bishop Robert Clarence (R.C.) Lawson, as well as Bishop Hubert Spencer and Apostle William Lee Bonner—three pioneer COOLJC leaders. In pursuing this history, I learned about the host of other men and women who helped lay its foundation and were instrumental in the evolution of this great church, for its history is a testament to the grace and power of God's providential expansion of His kingdom.

While the primary work of establishing the organization was blossoming, the church successfully navigated many challenges in its pursuit of the divine command to *"Go ye, and teach all nations, baptizing them in the name of the Father, and of the Son, and of the Holy Ghost: Teaching them to observe all things whatsoever I have commanded you: and, lo, I am with you always."* (Matt 28:19-20).

This chapter of his life was grounded in the word of God and was partly a function of Lawson's experiences as a black man in Louisiana during the post-reconstruction era, when black codes, the emergence and operation of the lynch mobs, and the Ku Klux Klan undermined black advancement from slavery. Lawson spoke of leaving Louisiana to escape a lynch mob.

This encounter led him to the Pentecostal Assemblies of the World, where he committed his life to Jesus, was baptized in Jesus' name, and received the baptism of the Holy Spirit. Yet, this spiritual experience did not obliterate the negative impact of the evils of white supremacy. Lawson coupled his knowledge of Scripture and gifts of oratory, leadership, and writing with a genuine compassion and love for his brothers and sisters in the church and community and a desire to address the evils of racism.

Justice in Jesus' Name is an attempt to illuminate Lawson's story, as well as the contributions of his mentee, Bishop Smallwood E. Williams, and fellow Apostolic leaders Reverend Dell Shields, Bishop Lawrence Campbell, Bishop James Parrott, his daughter, Joan Parrott, and a host of others.

Much of their social justice efforts evolved from benevolence ministries such as feeding programs and clothing distribution in which their congregations were engaged. These leaders' social engagement grew out of these ministries as they realized that, besides meeting immediate congregational and community needs, what was required was a radical change in the centers of power that resulted in poverty, housing inequality, economic and educational disparity, and other injustices. So, the leaders engaged in "doing justice" by taking a practical stand against inequality, and rampant oppression. These men and women worked tirelessly as activists to bring change to their local communities as well as to raise the consciousness of a nation mired in racism.

Their accounts offer irrefutable evidence that while Apostolic Pentecostal churches were very much "heavenly minded" they substantially engaged the realities of their time. But, in the end, I hope they will inspire a new generation of black Apostolic and other Pentecostals to confront the ongoing and seemingly irretractable challenges our communities still face.

Foreword

Small fires sometimes turn into conflagrations. So it was with the modern-day Pentecostal movement that began as a modest revival in the first decade of the last century, before becoming the most consequential movement within global Christianity. And black folk were at the center of this phenomenon. African Americans were also the leading actors in the schism that created the two major branches of the movement: Trinitarian and Oneness Pentecostalism. For over a century, the Trinitarians have comprised some seventy-five percent of the worldwide movement; the Jesus-only, Oneness, or Apostolic Pentecostals account for the remaining twenty-five percent.

Apostle James I. Clark, Jr., the author of this long-awaited book is an outstanding offspring of Apostolic Pentecostalism. He has been laboring in the ecclesiastical vineyard for a very, very long time. Now well into his eighth decade and still blessed with physical vigor and a powerful mind, he has had an amazing journey. A second-generation Apostolic pastor, following in the footsteps of his father, he has twice served as Presiding Apostle of the Church of Our Lord Jesus Christ, a major, black-led Apostolic denomination. The consummate prelate-scholar, Clark is a person of deep learning, with multiple degrees, including a Master of Divinity and two doctorates. It goes without saying that he is well acquainted with Christian theology in general and Pentecostal theology in particular.

First presented for his master's thesis at Union Theological Seminary over three decades ago, his work has been cited by many scholars within and outside the Pentecostal movement. Belatedly, but happily, it is now available in book form to larger audiences. This unique piece of scholarship is not a work of intellectual abstraction, emanating from the pen of some detached, dispassionate academic. No, Clark's approach is of a black Apostolic Pentecostal on fire. His three identities–black, Pentecostal, and Apostolic–are inseparable. Nor are they of recent vintage. And he writes from the trenches, bringing to his subject all the commitment and passion that only an insider of his caliber and experience could muster.

On its face, even Clark, a veteran Black Apostolic toiler, would seem to have a hard row to hoe. Pentecostals generally, Apostolics specifically, and black Apostolics, even more, have born the timeworn stereotype of being "too heavenly minded to be any earthly good." Clark disagrees, and this book bears witness against this received wisdom. For weighed in the balance of his research, the claim of social and political disengagement of the Black Apostolic tradition in the United States is wanting, incomplete and flawed.

This work of apologetics takes a largely biographical approach, using the involvement of men and women to highlight his thesis of the movement's commitment to social justice. For it is largely an account of COOLJC and its ecclesiastical diaspora, from the standpoint of the struggle for black social justice in the United States. Significantly, three of the four cases involve congregations and leaders affiliated with COOLJC's ecclesiastical diaspora. At the front of this impressive lineup is COOLJC founder, Robert Clarence Lawson, Garfield Thomas Haywood, his "father in the gospel," Smallwood Williams, pastor of one of the denomination's most dynamic congregations, and founder of Bible Way Church of Our Lord Jesus Christ.

While primarily concerned with practice or action, Clark's book is not devoid of thought, or theology. Yet as captured in its subtitle, "Early Black Apostolic Involvement in Civil Rights Struggles," Justice in Jesus' Name is only secondarily concerned with theology and doctrine. For the author establishes that the practice of Apostolics is a consequence of thought and their action flows directly from their theology. Their socio-political involvement and theology of liberation come out of their abiding Christology and Christ-centeredness, or their desire "to be like Jesus."

Altogether, Clark has made a signal contribution to the study of Apostolic Pentecostalism, theoretically as well as empirically. Theoretically, his book is a bold challenge to both the scholarly assertion and popular perception of the lack of relationship between black Apostolics and the struggle for black social justice in the United States. Empirically, this original work constitutes a primary source. Besides engaging with the secondary literature, its rich ethnography based on oral interviews with Apostolic notables will be a boon to future researchers and is the fruit of research that will inform Apostolic and Pentecostal scholarship far into the future. Clark has not labored in vain. Justice in Jesus' Name is at once a gem and a rock for the ages.

Michael O. West
Professor of African American Studies,
History, and African Studies
Pennsylvania State University

Introduction

This work attempts to respond to the often-uncomplimentary opinions of many writers, teachers, and religious leaders regarding the posture of the black Apostolic Pentecostal Church relative to the issue of social action. Nothing said here will silence many voices, for some are fixed in their opinions and will not change. For those who are willing to be fair, however, this work demonstrates how the black Apostolic tradition is well represented on the civil rights, social justice, and racial equality battlefield and, further, that this involvement is not of recent occurrence.

Since the inception of the Pentecostal Movement, there has been a profound sense that inequality among the races was unacceptable to God, and that racism, with its attendant ills, is to be fought and resisted. The primary basis for this perspective is the Pentecostal understanding of who Jesus is—especially among black Apostolic Pentecostals, sometimes referred to as Oneness Pentecostals. For us, Jesus is the Mighty God "in [whom] dwelleth all the fulness of the Godhead bodily" (Col

2:9). It was this Jesus who promised his disciples that they would "receive power after...the Holy Ghost...[came] upon [them]," (Acts 1:8) and that they would do "greater works" than he did when he was on earth (Jn 14:12).

With these and other empowering and liberating scriptures, black Apostolic Pentecostal leaders found the capacity to confront racial injustice and social evil in ways that made a difference. For many of them, the theology that the full presence of God dwells in the name and person of Jesus Christ empowered their dramatic, transformative response to social injustice and evil.

They acted not in the name of a "suffering savior," but of a sovereign God who, while present in the flesh, instructed his servants to "occupy [busy oneself with trade] till I come" (Lk 19:13). Thus, they saw themselves doing Kingdom work in the name of the Sovereign Lord who will return one day to judge between those who obey and those who disobey the Divine Imperative to serve the poor and oppressed (Matt 25:33).

After briefly referencing the 1906 Azusa Street Revival, this work looks at the origins of three predominant bodies within the black Apostolic tradition, The Pentecostal Assemblies of the World (PAW) is an antecedent of The Church of Our Lord Jesus Christ of the Apostolic Faith formed in New York City in 1919, and The Bible Way Church of Our Lord Jesus Christ World-Wide emerged from COOLJC in 1957.

Secondly, this work offers a brief analysis of the origin and content of the Oneness theology of the Godhead. This traces the emergence of the concept of the radical unity of God that resulted from attempting to harmonize the Trinitarian baptismal formula of Matthew 28:19 with the formula given by the Apostle Peter in Acts 2:38. A treatment of the "Theology of the Name" explores how this theology shaped the Apostolic understanding of the meaning and message of Jesus and the implications for their self-understanding and sense of mission among humankind.

This work presents interviews with black Apostolic leaders who were willing to share their motivation for involvement in the struggle for social change. It tells why they felt the burden to confront social evil as strongly as they felt the burden to preach to individuals about their personal need for salvation. Four case studies supported by these interviews demonstrate the thesis and highlight the underlying motivation for each person's actions.

Fourthly, my reflection on these cases offers an assessment of the weaknesses in the way social action has been carried out within the movement and offers a possible strategy for improving the quality of involvement in our urban centers. In addition, I suggest ways to make needed impact by establishing an ecumenical, extra-denominational conference of churches with the primary purpose of eliminating all forms of oppression. Unfortunately, I haven't developed a plan for formation of such an organization.

The refrain of a hymn. "To Be Like Him," I have heard and sung for most of my life captures the theme that has motivated and guided this work and those who made it possible:

> To be like Jesus, God's blessed Son,
> To be like Jesus, the Holy One,
> On Earth I long to be like Him
> All through life's journey
> From Earth to glory
> I only ask, to be like Him.

Lee Roy Ooton , 1923[1]

---

[1] Lee Roy Ooton, "To be like Jesus" *The Bridegroom Songs, Bethlehem Temple ed.* Detroit, MI: The Voice in the Wilderness Publishers, n.d., 71.

CHAPTER 1

The Origin of the Black Apostolic Tradition

First Stages

As with most factions of the Pentecostal movement, the black Apostolic tradition traces its origin to the great Los Angeles revival at 312 Azusa Street in 1906. The revival started from "cottage prayer meetings" in the home of Richard and Ruth Asberry in the winter and early spring of that year. The leader was a black elder named William Joseph Seymour who was active in the Holiness movement. Prior to coming to Los Angeles, he had served as an interim pastor of a small church in Houston, Texas. There, he was exposed to the teaching of Charles Fox Parham, the founder of the Apostolic Faith movement, a group that claimed as many as 13,000 members in the south-central region of the United States.[1]

Leaders of the Apostolic Faith movement taught that Holy Spirit baptism, with the initial evidence of glossolalia (speaking in tongues), "was an experience subsequent to conversion that every Christian should seek."[2] They explained that this experience was like what the Lord's disciples experienced on the day of Pentecost in Jerusalem. Hence, they label it the "Pentecostal Experience."[3]

While in Houston, Seymour attended Parham's Bible school. Though he was not allowed to sit in the classroom with white students but had to listen to the lectures from outside the door, he embraced Parham's teaching[4] and took the message to Los Angeles where he had been invited to preach as a pastoral

---

[1] Cecil M. Robeck, Jr., "Azusa Street Revival," in Stanley M. Burgess, Gary B. McGee, and Patrick H. Alexander, eds, *Dictionary of Pentecostal and Charismatic Movements*. Grand Rapids, MI: Regency Reference Library, Zondervan Publishing House, 1988, 31.

[2] H. Vinson Synan, "Seymour, William Joseph (1870-1922)," in Burgess et al. eds. *Dictionary of Pentecostal and Charismatic Movements*, 780. Synan notes that this was known as Classical Pentecostal Theology and Charles Fox Parham is credited with its initial formulation in 1902. For this reason, many white Pentecostals insist that, he, not Seymour, should be regarded as the founder of the modern Pentecostal Movement.

[3] Ibid., 780-781. Unlike Charismatics, early Pentecostals made a distinction between the regenerating of the Holy Spirit and its ministry. The evidence that one had been empowered by the Spirit was the experience of speaking in tongues, or glossolalia, an event that became known as the "initial evidence."

[4] Ibid. Parham was a segregationist and did not allow Seymour to sit in the classroom with the white students. Nevertheless, Seymour accepted what he learned from the hallway. He embraced the teaching, although, at the time, he personally had not experienced glossolalia.

candidate.[5] The Pentecostal message, that one must speak in tongues as evidence of receiving the Holy Spirit, was unacceptable to pastor Julia W. Hutchins, and Seymour was locked out of the church. This turn of events placed him in the Asberrys' Bonnie Brae Street home.[6] H. Vinson Synan reports on the situation this way:

> After several weeks of prayer meetings in the Asberrys' home, Seymour and others received the sought-for tongues experience, an event that sparked an intense revival. For a time, services were held on the couple's front porch, where Seymour preached to crowds gathered in the streets. As the numbers increased, larger quarters were needed. A search of the downtown area of Los Angeles turned up an old building at 312 Azusa Street that had formerly been an African Methodist Episcopal Church but had been more recently used as a stable and warehouse.[7]

Leonard Lovett indicates that Seymour's response to the "bolted door" was to hold cottage meetings which the Lord miraculously transformed into "a gateway for the international Pentecostal movement."[8] People from around the world visited the mission and shared in this great outpouring of the Holy

---

[5] Ibid. A young woman named Neely Terry encouraged Seymour to make the trip to Los Angeles. The pastor of the church he went to serve was Julia W. Hutchins.

[6] Leonard Lovett, "Black Origins of the Pentecostal Movement," in Vinson Synan, ed., *Aspects of Pentecostal Charismatic Origins*. Plainfield, NJ: Logos International, 1975, 138.

[7] Synan, "Seymour, William Joseph," 780.

[8] Lovett, "Black Origins of the Pentecostal Movement."

Spirit.[9] Besides the experience of glossolalia, another unusual phenomenon was taking place. At this time, the Azusa Mission was interracial and non-sexist.[10] Cecil Robeck, Jr. credits Seymour with "providing the vision of a truly color-blind congregation."[11] While the experiment of racial inclusion was short-lived, the revival intensified over the next few years, with the most dramatic period being between 1906 and 1908.[12]

Soon, there was a proliferation of Pentecostal groups throughout the South and West, with several missions opening in the Los Angeles area. They formed some of these new congregations because of the unwillingness of their white members to continue under the leadership of a black man.[13] Others formed out of fear that the "movement" would become cold and formal like the Holiness Movement, which was more acceptable to the mainline churches. Frank Bartleman, an early

---

[9] Ibid. Lovett quotes Seymour from "Pentecost Has Come," *The Apostolic Faith* 1:1 September 1906, 1, when he heralds the great outpouring of the Holy Spirit, saying, "God makes no difference in nationality. Ethiopians, Chinese, Indians, Mexicans, and other nationalities worship together. The people are melted together 100 made one lump, one bread, all one body in Christ Jesus."

[10] Synan, "Seymour, William Joseph," 780.

[11] Robeck, "Azusa Street Revival," 36. See also Iain MacRobert, *Black Roots and White Racism in Early Pentecostalism in the USA*. New York: St. Martin's Press, 1988, 82. He says the "interracial phenomenon occurred at a most inopportune time and involved the least likely of persons, as far as the racial climate in the country was concerned. It occurred in the years of America's most racist period, those from 1890-1920... Even more significant is the fact that this interracial accord took place among the very groups that had traditionally been most at odds, poor [white and black people]."

[12] Synan, "Seymour, William Joseph," 780.

[13] Ibid.

participant in the revival, left the Azusa Street Mission because he did not believe they should have a formal organization.[14]

All that was new and exciting about the Azusa Street Revival changed after 1908. Doctrinal disagreements such as the "Finished Work controversy" caused breaches between Seymour and several of the movement's more popular preachers. William Durham, the doctrine's major proponent, argued that the "finished work" of Christ on Calvary becomes available to the believer at the time of justification. Unlike most Pentecostals of his day, Durham reasoned that "the benefits of Calvary are therefore appropriated for sanctification over the entire period of the Christian's life rather than at a single subsequent moment."[15] This teaching renounced the Wesleyan Holiness doctrine of sanctification as a "second work of grace."[16]

Other disagreements hastened the cooling of the revival's fires, but its work had been accomplished, and Pentecostal teaching was rapidly spreading across the nation and the world. In Robeck's words,

> Internationally, the message spread rapidly as people who believed themselves to have been freshly touched by the Spirit, and in many cases to have been given a gift of

---

[14] Robeck, "Azusa Street Revival," 31-32. Bartleman became an itinerant evangelist after fellowshipping with the Azusa Street Mission from 1906-1908. He was a journalist and did much to promote the revival.

[15] Synan, "Seymour, William Joseph," 781. (See 780-781 for background on William H. Durham and the "finished work" controversy and confrontation.)

[16] Ibid., 781.

languages (tongues) for missionary work, went abroad. Lucy Leatherman made a trip around the world, while Frank Bartleman circled the globe once and made a second two-year evangelistic tour to Europe. Thomas Junk, as well as Bernt and Magna Berntsen, went from Azusa to China. M. L. Ryan led several young people to missions in the Philippines, Japan, and Hong Kong. The George E. Bergs, and the A. G. Garrs went to India, while Tom Hezmalhalch and John G. Lake went to South Africa. Pastor A. H. Post became a long-term missionary to Egypt; and a host of people, mostly black, including Edward and Mollie McGauley, G. W. and Daisy Batman, and Julia W. Hutchins took the Pentecostal message to Liberia.[17]

Many who experienced the baptism of the Holy Spirit sought to fulfill the Lord's command, to his disciples in Acts 1:8, in which he said, *"ye shall be [my] witnesses… into the uttermost part of the earth."*

On the domestic scene, among the many groups that formed several growing Apostolic Faith missions was the Pentecostal Assemblies of the World.[18] This then Trinitarian body held its first-recorded meeting in 1907 in Los Angeles. Stephen Jacob Jackson (J. J.) Frazee served as its first secretary from 1912 to 1916. Garfield Thomas (G. T.) Haywood, a prominent black leader of the Apostolic Faith Assembly in Indianapolis, Indiana,

---

[17] Robeck, "Azusa Street Revival," 36.
[18] Ibid.

held credentials with the body beginning in 1911.[19] This group became the largest of the Pentecostal body to respond to the "New Issue."[20]

The New Issue

An international revival was convened in 1913 at Arroyo Seco outside Los Angeles, with prominent evangelist Maria Woodworth-Etter as the featured revivalist. For most of the meeting, nothing out of the ordinary occurred, until R. E. McAlister preached a baptismal sermon in which he announced that the proper formula for water baptism was in the name of Jesus Christ.[21]

While many heard this idea with some interest,[27] one attendee, John G. Scheppe, "was inspired to study and pray about this teaching throughout the night. Early the next morning, he ran through the camp, shouting that the Lord had revealed the truth on baptism in the name of Jesus Christ to him. Not long after listening to his revelation, many believed."[22]

Among those who accepted and taught this new understanding were many Assemblies of God (AG) members who had

---

[19] David A. Reed, "Pentecostal Assemblies of the World," in Stanley M. Burgess, et al., *Dictionary of Pentecostal and Charismatic Movements*, 1988, 700.

[20] David A. Reed, "Oneness Pentecostalism" in Burgess, et al., *Dictionary of Pentecostal and Charismatic Movements*, 646.

[21] Ibid., 644.

[22] Ibid.

previously held to the Trinitarian baptism formula.[23] According to David A. Reed, by spring 1915, the new understanding was spreading rapidly among its members.[24] The aggressiveness of these new converts and the rapidity with which their views were being accepted soon caused concern within the fledgling body. Assemblies of God leaders challenge this doctrine, mainly because New Issue advocates insisted that any believer who had not been baptized in Jesus's name had to be re-baptized.[25]

What panicked the Assemblies of God members was the rebaptism of one of its prominent leaders, Eudorus N. Bell, who was a member of the Executive Presbytery and editor of its two magazines, *Weekly Evangel* and *Word and Witness*. In reaction to this, J. Roswell Flower, Bell's assistant editor, directly challenged New Issue advocates and moved the Presbytery to call a meeting to "examine the issue and stabilize the Assemblies of God."[26] The most this meeting achieved was a strained and tentative truce.[27]

New Issue advocates pursued their course and, while making inroads into AG membership, began questioning the Trinitarian view of the Godhead. By the fourth General Council in the fall

---

[23] Ibid.

[24] Ibid.

[25] Ibid. Although Haywood was not a card-carrying member of the Assemblies of God, he had a strong relationship with many of their churches around the country. The leaders were surprised when he and 485 of his members left to join the new movement.

[26] Ibid. and Gary B. McGee, "Flower, Joseph James Roswell (1888-1970)" in Burgess, et.al., 312.

[27] Ibid.

of 1916, Assemblies of God leaders confronted these advocates with a sixteen-point `Statement of Fundamental Truths' that included a strongly worded affirmation of the traditional Trinitarian doctrine. Oneness proponents would not bend, however, and after the vote was taken for the adoption of the statement, 156 of the 585 ministers and many congregations were barred from membership.[28]

Now two issues—rebaptism and nature of the Godhead—put this denomination on the collision course to schism. Many have speculated that, had these two issues not been so strongly held and pushed by the Oneness advocates, the Assemblies' acceptance of the Apostolic formula as an alternative baptismal formula would have settled the matter.

Several ministers who left the denomination emerged as leaders[29] in a new Oneness organization, the General Assembly of the Apostolic Assemblies. This body was formed in Eureka Springs, Arkansas, on December 28, 1916, with 154 ministers, missionaries, elders, deacons, and evangelists.[30]

The effort was short-lived, however, since the organization was not authorized by the United States government to issue credentials to its ministers. This made them eligible for the draft.[31]In January 1918, Haywood intervened and facilitated a merger between the General Assembly of the Apostolic Assemblies and the Pentecostal Assemblies of the World under

---

[28] Ibid.
[29] Ibid.
[30] Reed "Oneness Pentecostalism."
[31] Ibid.

the PAW charter."[32] With this move, again, Oneness Pentecostals seemed to have forged an integrated fellowship. Yet within a short time, the tenacious and sinister evil of racism prevailed when white ministers feared black domination. It was not long before a schism resulted.[33]

Apparently, this rupture was precipitated by the decision to move the headquarters of the Pentecostal Assemblies of the World to Indianapolis. Haywood, an Indianapolis resident, and the only black member of the three-person Board of Directors, served as the general secretary for the organization. With the move to his hometown, his tremendous leadership and preaching ability, and perhaps, his status as a recognized official, the complexion of the Pentecostal Assemblies of the World changed significantly. It was no longer a predominantly white organization; black people represented the greater portion of its membership.[34]

This shift in demographics proved more than the white membership could handle. The preponderance of black ministers meant that most of the committees and offices were held by the blacks.[35] In November 1922—only five years after PAW was organized—the southern white churches held their own segregated "Southern Bible Conference."[36] Soon after, they

---

[32] Ibid.
[33] Ibid.
[34] Ibid.
[35] MacRobert, 72. He states that at the first meeting in 1918, no black members were present, but when a second meeting was held in 1919, the office of secretary passed from William Booth-Clibbon, a white man to Haywood.
[36] Ibid.

insisted that their fellowship cards be signed by the white leaders, asserting that this demand was "because of Jim Crow pressures in the South."[37] What they could not answer for the black brothers was how anyone would know the signer's race.

The split came at the 1924 PAW Annual Convention, and after that, there were two major Oneness organizations—the Pentecostal Assemblies of the World and the Apostolic Assemblies General Association.[38] Haywood became the presiding bishop of the PAW and served until his death due to a heart attack in 1931.

After he died, white ministers again attempted to unify all Oneness groups that had formed between 1924 and 1931, offering a" racially balanced, integrated structure" that many blacks eagerly embraced. Yet, several black leaders feared that insincerity and opportunism were the motives prompting the white negotiators. Despite their concerns, in a swift merger in November 1931, a new body was formed under the name, The Pentecostal Assemblies of Jesus Christ."[39]

Reed explains that the changes, the compromise to change the name of the organization, and the abandonment of the episcopal form of government practiced since 1925 were sufficient reasons for ministers like Samuel Grimes, E. F. Akers, and A. W. Lewis to take action.[40] A reorganization meeting was called in Dayton, Ohio, and PAW re-emerged as a

---

[37] Ibid.
[38] Ibid.
[39] Reed, "Oneness Pentecostalism," 646.
[40] Ibid.

predominantly black body with Grimes as its leader: and so, the black Apostolic tradition had its beginnings.[41]

CHAPTER 2

Oneness Theology: An Overview

Again, three factors gave birth to the black Oneness movement we know today: the "New Issue" of the appropriate baptismal formula, the new understanding of the Godhead, and the racism that manifested itself in white members' unwillingness to be under black leadership.

The notion that "God is one God" and not three was the main theological concern of Oneness advocates. Trinitarian believers saw Oneness advocates as denying the existence of the Father and the Holy Spirit. So, they marshaled resources to correct what they saw as an awful error, and the battle lines were drawn.

McAlister's New Issue was based on the conclusion of Peter's sermon in Acts 2:38:

And Peter said to them, 'Repent and be baptized every one of you in the name of Jesus Christ for the forgiveness of your sins; and you shall receive the gift of the Holy Spirit.'

His revelation generated enthusiastic endorsement by many people who excitedly shared the new formula for baptism. Frank Ewart, a preacher who attended the Azusa Street Revival in its later years, pondered the matter more fully than some others. After meeting with McAlister, he reported that McAlister's argument was that,

Lord, Jesus, Christ, was the counterpart of Father, Son, and Holy Ghost, made Jesus' words in Matthew 28:19, one of those parabolic statements of truth, which was interpreted in Acts 2:38 and other scriptures.[1]

In Ewart's words,

Long after the meeting with…McAlister…I received the revelation…of the absolute deity of our Lord Jesus Christ and saw that as all the fullness of the Godhead dwelling in Jesus bodily, baptism, as the Apostles administered it, in the name of the Lord Jesus Christ, was the one and only fulfillment of Matthew 28:19.[2]

As Ewart saw it, any other form of baptism missed the mark. Thus, the impetus for change had been unleashed, but in that short time, a good deal more had developed in the thinking of Ewart and others. According to Reed, when Ewart preached his

---

[1] Reed, "Aspects of the Origins of Oneness Pentecostalism" in Vinson Synan, ed., *Aspect of Pentecostal Charismatic Origins*, 146.

[2] Ibid.

first sermon concerning the new concept, this formula received its full theological justification in a unitarian concept of God.[3] But this account only describes the events that gave birth to this concept and facilitated its promulgation throughout the modern Pentecostal movement. In discovering how this idea "took hold" and flourished so readily, some interesting themes emerged.

Some suggest that the antecedents of the Oneness Pentecostal movement were in the Great Awakenings and the 19th-century Holiness Movements. The spirit of 19th-century revivalism, with its emphasis on "independence, pragmatism, and concern for the common person freed people to explore and express innovative religious insights and experiences. This same spirit that produced the "religion of the heart" gave birth to the Oneness revelation. According to Reed,

> Scheppe, Ewart and others were motivated not by cold logic but by a heartfelt devotion to Christ and the Bible. Commenting on the new revelation, Ewart observed: 'mere intellect cannot open the treasury of the Name of God.' God speaks to the heart. If the heart is dead, the Name is sealed.[4]

This was an indictment against those who held the Trinitarian view who were often accused of following "man's religion" rather than following Christ. The notion that one cannot understand the Oneness of the Godhead unless it is revealed by

---

[3] Ibid.
[4] Ibid., 154.

the Lord Jesus Christ himself is held as firmly today by most Oneness advocates as it was then. For them, failure to embrace this position was evidence that one had not heard from God.

Finally, a heavy Christo centrism in the millenarian movement of the 19th century emphasized the Second Coming of Jesus Christ and the saints' reign on earth with Him.[63] This emphasis brought about "a shift in revivalistic piety from orthodox creeds and speculation on the Trinity to a full-orbed Christo centrism in worship, thought, and practice."[5]

This is the climate into which the new concept was planted. What remained for those who advocated the new baptism formula was reconciling it with the Matthew 28:19 commission, and Ewart set out to do that. What emerged from his efforts was a rejection of any teaching that suggested Jesus was less than full Deity.[6] It was felt that Trinitarians, in addition to advocating tritheism, (three distinct persons in the Godhead) also subordinated Jesus—or God the Son—to God the Father and God the Holy Spirit, because only one third of the Godhead became incarnate." This understanding caused Ewart and his supporters to argue Trinitarian viewed Jesus as neither the full revelation of the Deity nor the revelation of the Full Deity.[7]

For Oneness advocates, no view short of a literal understanding of Colossians 2:9, "in him dwelleth all the fulness of the Godhead bodily," was acceptable. Ewart was attacking a view

---

[5] Ibid., 157.
[6] Ibid., 148.
[7] Ibid.

that rendered Jesus less than absolute God when he wrote that he had received the revelation of the "absolute deity of the Lord Jesus Christ."[8]

Andrew D. Urshan, another prominent Oneness leader, attacked what he viewed as the subordination of Christ, asserting that,

> In these days of ours, not only are thousands of Christians denying the absolute Deity of our Lord, but those who believed it are trying to preach him feebly as God the Son, and by so doing they think they have gone to the limit of exalting 'the Lord of glory.'[9]

What was driving this issue for Oneness Pentecostals, then, was the perceived neglect of the importance of the name of God as set forth in the Old Testament. Reed explains,

> God was known to His covenant people through the revealing of his name. His nature was so bound up with His name that the revealed name of God, YHWH, was as sacred as Yahweh Himself, worthy of adoration and pregnant with divine power. God's giving of His name was, in fact, an act of giving of Himself because it was only through His name that He was known.[10]

This was the hermeneutical principle employed by Oneness advocates. When they spoke of Jesus, they ascribed all

---

[8] Ibid.
[9] Ibid.
[10] Ibid., 148-149.

messianic prophecies to Him, and "transferred to him all the prerogatives and characteristics of God."[11] Thus, for them, Jesus of Nazareth, the Son of Mary, "is not the Incarnation of the Second Person of the Trinity but the FULL revelation of the one God of Israel, who's finally revealed name for this dispensation is Jesus."[12]

Oneness teaching is also referred to as a "Jewish-Christian Theology of the Name."[13] From this designation, three specifically Jewish beliefs emerge:

1. that the name of God reveals God's true nature,

2. that in God's being, God is radically one; and

3. that God 'dwells' in 'tabernacles,' temples and, in His Name.[14]

The understanding "that the name JESUS is a major Christological designation connoting his Deity" is developed from the third concept. This is why Ewart insisted that "the unity of God is sustained by the absolute unity or oneness of His name."[15]

The unitarian Pentecostal concept of the Godhead gets at how Oneness theology shaped its social consciousness and action.

---

[11] Ibid. See also Vinson Synan, "Pentecostalism," in *Aspects of Pentecostal Charismatic Origins*, 83.

[12] Reed, "Aspects of the Origins of Oneness Pentecostalism," 7, 148-149.

[13] Reed, "Oneness Pentecostalism," 648.

[14] Ibid.

[15] Ibid.

Though this conception argues against the Trinity as understood by its adherents, it does not deny the Father and the Holy Spirit. Haywood clarified this point by explaining,

> There is no one who knows the Word of God, and has been baptized in Jesus' name, that denies the Father and the Son. They acknowledge the Father and the Son in Christ Jesus, The Fatherhood of God is found only in the Son, who was God manifested in the flesh.[16]

This soon was called the 'Jesus only' perspective while Jesus 'filled all and in all.' Thus, for Oneness advocates, 'Jesus in his person and name [is] the revealer of the whole Godhead.' For them, "the name of Jesus 'etymologically embodies the name of Yahweh,' and Yahweh points to yet a further revelation of the name of God." Again, 'the name of Jesus is regarded as the proper name of God for this age, reveals the identity of Jesus, and describes His function as Saviour of the world.'[17]

Black Apostolics embraced this "theology of the Name of Jesus" and thus advocated a Christology that shapes and defines every facet of their lives. Their sermons, songs, writings, testimonies, etc. all focused on Jesus as the Mighty God.

Songs like "To Be Like Him" express this perspective. A cursory review of the popular songbooks of the black Apostolic movement reinforces this point. In one of the most popular of

---

[16] Reed, "Aspects of the Origins of Oneness Pentecostalism," 150.
[17] Ibid., 149, 160.

Haywood's songbooks, *The Bridegroom Songs,*[18] forty-five out of ninety-four songs are about Jesus. These include such titles as, "The Power in Jesus's Name," "Do All in Jesus's Name," "His Name Should Be Praised," "Jesus," "Jesus is Faithful," "Jesus is First of All," "Jesus the Rock of Ages," "Jesus, the Son of God," "Jesus Our All in All," "The Life-Giving Name," and "My God, I Know His Name."

The chorus to this song reads:

Jesus, Jesus,
No other name has been given to save us;
But Jesus, Jesus,
My God I know His Name. [19]

Another song entitled "The Name of God" by Haywood and Fern Reneich Smith has as its fifth stanza:

Manna true came down from heaven,
Bearing with it Jesus's name,
Held in mystery through the ages;
Now tis spoken clear and plain;

Christ in you, the hope of glory,
Lord of heaven, Lord of hosts;
And in Jesus is the name
of Father, Son, and Holy Ghost.

---

[18] G. T. Haywood, *The Bridegroom Songs. Bethlehem Temple edition.* (Detroit, MI: The Voice in the Wilderness Publishers, s.d.

[19] Garfield Thomas Haywood "My God, I Know His Name." *The Bridegroom Songs,* 3.

And its chorus relates:

> Jesus is the Lord of Glory
> And was when on earth He trod.
> Jesus, everlasting Father,
> Jesus is the name of God.[20]

This high Christology is the primary influence on the activities of Oneness leaders. While I remember hearing only part of the often-repeated scripture "Whatsoever you do in word or deed, do all in the name of the Lord Jesus," rarely did I hear the latter portion, "giving thanks to God and the Father by him," expressed (Col 3:17).

It then comes as no surprise that every person I interviewed eventually stressed the life and teachings of Jesus as the primary reason they were engaged in social action. Inevitably, they would quote Luke 4:18-19, or say, "This is what Jesus did, and we are supposed to be like Jesus."

I first interviewed Dr. Del Shields, the Pastor of Zion Gospel Assembly in Jamaica, Queens, New York. He was a top-ranked DJ for the New York metropolitan area's gospel radio station WWRL, and host for "In the Sanctuary," a community affairs program.

> CLARK. Dr. Shields, would you say the church in which you grew up was a socially conscious church?

---

[20] Garfield Thomas Haywood and Fern Reneich Smith "The Name of God" *The Bridegroom Songs*, 12.

SHIELDS. It's very possible that we were very socially conscious without being socially aware. People always brought clothes to the church; food was always available. When someone went to the hospital, automatically people in the church had to go by that house and take care of the washing of clothing and preparing of food. I guess it was a kind of program without knowing it and I think that we were taught that this was the way of life, you could not be saved, you could not be a member of the church, *you certainly could not be a follower of Jesus Christ if you were not willing to give what you had.* (Emphasis mine.)

CLARK. Was this done only for members of the church?

SHIELDS. No, anyone came in. When it came to food and clothing... remember at that time the demographics were much different from what they are now, in that your members were around the corner— within walking distance.

CLARK. Did you have people driving from Brooklyn or other sections of Queens?

SHIELDS. No, not at that time, because we didn't have cars—that came much later. I think you grew up with the sense *you could always relate to your Sunday school lessons when Jesus was busy healing folk, feeding folk—well that's what you were doing, that's what we're supposed to do, and our lives are... it was a very simple theology but a very effective theology.* (Emphasis mine.)

CLARK. So, you're saying that this social activity was driven by the teaching of the scripture, the theology or teaching of the church.

SHIELDS: Always. When I had Catholic friends, and these Catholic friends were part of the Catholic Youth Organization and they had Catholic Charities and what not, there was something that the church did. Their church fed the hungry and so forth, *but in our situation, it was Jesus who did the feeding, Jesus who did the clothing. So, there's a big difference, and I think it was always funny to me how they could always relate to the pope, that he was the spokesman for Christ, the director, and I'm saying, 'Well, if this man was in our church, we wouldn't have to go through anybody.'* (i.e., to get to Jesus. Emphasis mine.)[21]

In another interview with Bishop Norman Quick of the Church of God in Christ, he tells a story that reinforces the point Dr. Shields is making when he states, "It was Jesus who did the feeding, Jesus who did the clothing." In Bishop Quick's words,

One little anecdote has it that a lady prayed for some help and the local numbers runner brought the food and the people tried to make her deny that God had delivered her,

---

[21] Interview with Rev Dr. Del Shields, February 19, 1990.

but she stood fast and said God sent it even if the devil brought it.[22]

This indicates what Pentecostals and Apostolics mean when they ascribe a blessing or work to God or Jesus. Jesus makes the blessing possible, although he uses human instrumentalities. Further on in our interview, Dr. Shields said he thanked God for his Pentecostal background. I asked him why. He gave me a rather lengthy but useful explanation.

> I believe very strongly, my theology is very simple, 'my hope is built on nothing less than Jesus's blood and righteousness.' I know—how could I go from being the number one jazz disc jockey in New York City, which is the number one market, to now becoming the number one gospel disc jockey? This just doesn't happen unless God is in it. My Pentecostalism, my training, is that we're to be like Jesus, we're to emulate Him, we're to do everything as He would do it. So, he fed the hungry and we tried to feed the hungry. He clothed the naked and we tried to clothe the naked. He said, 'The poor you'll have with you always,' but he didn't mean that the poor couldn't work— so these facilities are available within the church context, and I say to the people, 'why not use them?'[23]

---

[22] Interview with Bishop Norman Quick, March 1990.
[23] Ibid.

He goes on to talk about how he used his show to connect people with job opportunities and a wide range of other services.

My interview with Bishop Smallwood E. Williams, Presiding Apostle of the 500,000-member International Bible Way Church World-Wide, and senior pastor of the 2,400-member Bible Way Church of Our Lord Jesus Christ in Washington, DC, was revealing as well:

> CLARK. Bishop, your activities for the cause of social justice and racial equality are so well known, one need only mention your name around this area, and someone will recognize you for some help you've given. Little is known about your motivation, why you have done and are doing the fine things you do. Would you tell me something about that?

> WILLIAMS. The social action portion of my ministry is based on the scripture so well known to you and others. The ministry of the Lord Jesus Christ—began in his hometown, in the city of Nazareth—the city where he was brought up. It was an environment that was atypical to the kind of situation where people would have social problems, and it says here: [he takes the Bible and turns to and reads Luke 4:18-19]. Now, there is involved in here a basic recognition of the needs of the people. 'The rich he sent away empty and the poor he sent away full.' So, it is quite natural: in fact, I think

that all ministers, especially black ministers and those of other underprivileged areas and groups in which economic barriers exist, need to be interested in 'give us our daily bread,' because you can't have a real life without the necessities of life that are spoken of here.[24]

Here again, the life of Jesus is referenced and seen as giving His true disciples a mandate to "go and do likewise." These interview excerpts illustrate the importance of the Apostolic perspective of the teaching of the scripture, Jesus the Christ, and the importance of both for their self-understanding and activity in the world.

This self-understanding leads us to question, if this high Christology and Word-centeredness fundamentally influenced black Apostolics' responsiveness to racism and social injustices, why were white Apostolics not similarly influenced? In all fairness, some were, but just a few were—too few to make a difference. Historians have attempted to exonerate the white Apostolics who failed to prevent racist schisms that resulted from the pressure of Jim Crow laws. They use this as an excuse for their failure to act, but their arguments are unconvincing.

From my perspective, the black Apostolic response is no different than those offered to explain the emergence of black independent churches and denominations. The secondary point of this work is that social action is generic to the black church tradition. To different degrees, black Apostolic and

---

[24] Interview with Bishop Smallwood E. Williams, February 8, 1990.

other black Pentecostals have been full participants of that arena.

Black Apostolics, like black brothers and sisters in other denominations, were (and are) the oppressed, and thus are unavoidably involved in dealing with oppression. They were thus enabled, by their existential situation and the Holy Spirit, to see and hear the gospel in ways that their victimizers could not. in his essay, "Doing Theology in a Situation of Conflict," Frank Chikane quotes Dr. Allan Boesak,

> One cannot 'do theology' without being involved with the experiences of actual struggles, sufferings, and joys of particular communities.[25]

Thus, the black Apostolic understanding of the Christ and the Word intersected with their existential reality and "called forth" from them a prophetic word and concrete social action against the social evils and injustices they and their neighbors faced.

The following chapters show how each person addressed their situation in the way they considered best. They saw themselves as acting in concert with Jesus Christ to transform it. They were not deluded into believing they could "save the world," nor were they "so heavenly-minded that they were of no earthly good." Rather, they were fully engaged in doing what they could, knowing that they were joining Jesus the Christ who is

---

[25] Frank Chikane, "Doing Theology in a Situation of Conflict," in Charles Villa-Vicencio and John W. de Gruchy, eds., *Resistance and Hope: South African Essays in Honor of Beyers Naude.* Grand Rapids, MI: Wm B. Eerdmans, 1985, 99.

on the "side of the downtrodden and the poor." They sought to "bring about a more humane and just society—the kingdom of God."[26]

---

[26] Ibid, 102.

CHAPTER 3

Apostolics "Doing Theology"

Bishop Robert Clarence Lawson

In 1913, Robert Clarence (R.C.) Lawson entered the fellowship of the Apostolic Faith Assembly pastored by Garfield Thomas Haywood.[1] In doing so, he became a member of the Pentecostal Assemblies of the World (PAW) when the denomination was experiencing its most exciting period. Lawson started preaching shortly after receiving the baptism of the Holy Spirit. Between 1913 and 1919, when he left Indianapolis for New York, Lawson founded churches in San Antonio, Texas, St. Louis, Missouri and Columbus, Ohio. As a General Elder of

---

[1] Mabel Thomas and Robert C. Spellman, *The Life, Legend, and Legacy of Bishop R. C. Lawson.* New York: By authors, 1983, 69.

PAW, the energetic and talented young minister had authority over these churches.

During that time, Haywood, his "father in the gospel"[2] served as PAW General Secretary. Again, the organization was beginning to experience racial tensions that led to a painful split in 1924. This experience had a profound impact on Lawson, who had experienced similar racial prejudice previously, having to leave the place of his birth, New Iberia, Louisiana, because "a white posse was after him."[3]

That the experience, which probably occurred when he was in his mid- to late teens, influenced his thinking until his conversion is evidenced by an anecdote recorded in *The Life, Legend, and Legacy of Bishop R. C. Lawson*. It recalls an encounter with a white Christian man who tried to witness to him concerning salvation:

> Well, I didn't want to hear anything from him because I was from the South and hadn't gotten the negatives of segregation out of me yet, and how they treated me down there. And I didn't believe there could be a God when they had such prejudice in their minds. So, I let all my feelings about the evils of the South fall on this old man. I just counted him as one of them. I talked to him in a very ugly way, and finally he got up and walked away.[4]

---

[2] Ibid., 41.
[3] Ibid.
[4] Ibid.

After his salvation experience and exposure to Haywood's leadership as a strong advocate for racial integration, Lawson's perspective changed significantly. That may explain his uniqueness as a progressive Apostolic Pentecostal minister, whose strong social concern found such dramatic and concrete expression in his life and work in New York City from as early as the 1920s.

At a time when the South was succumbing to the imposition of Jim Crow laws and humiliating, terrorizing, and murdering its black citizens, the Pentecostal Assemblies of the World was a multiracial body struggling to preserve its uniqueness as it believed God willed it. The courage of the PAW black members to stand in the face of increasing racial prejudice had to impress young Lawson, a leader with a vision of his own.[5]

He developed a deep appreciation for the talents and abilities of black leadership in the organization. The publications and songs of Haywood and others influenced him and may have inspired two of his more important writings: *The Anthropology of Jesus Christ, Our Kinsman* and *An Open Letter to a Southern White Minister on Prejudice.* The work was written in 1925 and the latter in 1949. The first treatise delineates how the bloodline of Jesus Christ runs back to Ham, the father of the black race.[6] The second is an effective polemic against the doctrine of white

    [5] Morris E. Golder, *History of the Pentecostal Assemblies of the World. Indianapolis: Pentecostal Assemblies of the World.* Indianapolis, IN: Pentecostal Assemblies of the World, 1973, 43-45.
    [6] Robert C. Lawson, *The Anthropology of Jesus Christ Our Kinsman.* Piqua, OH: Ohio Ministries, 1925.

supremacy that was being advocated by most southern white churchmen at the time.[7]

Haywood, his spiritual father, demonstrated a strong interest in church and community people and assisted them with concerns that were more than just spiritual. As Morris Golder explains his approach,

> He not only aided members of the 'household of faith,' but he willingly helped others who appealed to him. Brother Haywood proved that he believed it is more blessed to give than to receive and that the highest joy in life is in the service of others.[8]

An example of this commitment was exhibited in a September 25, 1932, church bulletin which devoted a paragraph to the need to support a ministry to local prisons. On the back was an announcement regarding "The People's Burial Company, Inc.," which Haywood owned. Its services were opened to people who could not afford the more costly services offered by other morticians. Its logo reappeared in 1950 as the "People's Funeral Homes" which Lawson operated in New York.

Lawson brought this spirit with him when he arrived in the city broke, without a residence, but burning with a zeal to do the Lord's work. All that follows would give testimony to his success and strong commitment to social action. It was a commitment that went quite a distance to make life more

---

[7] Robert C. Lawson, *An Open Letter to a Southern White Minister on Prejudice, s.l.: s.n, s.d.*

[8] Golder, *History of the Pentecostal Assemblies of the World,* 43-45.

bearable for the people in his congregation and those in the community of Harlem, New York. The first and longest lasting project he undertook was the R.C. Lawson Institute in Southern Pines, North Carolina.

This Institute was originally called the Industrial Union Institute and Training School.[9] The property is believed to have been donated by the city.[10] According to an article in the *New York Amsterdam News*, "the school, [served] as a combination high school and home for children from crowded city homes."[11] In an earlier souvenir journal, the Church of Our Lord Jesus Christ wrote concerning the school:

> The R.C. Lawson Institute has become a boon to working parents who desire supervision of their children while they are away from home during the day. Children are admitted from preschool age through high school, at a rather low tuition rate. As a matter of fact, the cost is $9.00 per week, and this includes board, lodging and tuition.[12]

The article reports that these children came from various denominations.

---

[9] Thomas and Spellman, *The Life, Legend, and Legacy of Bishop R. C. Lawson*, 41.

[10] "A Brief History of Refuge Temple," *Founders Day Souvenir Journal*, August 25, 1944.

[11] "Harlem's Refuge Temple Hails 38th Anniversary." *The New York Amsterdam News*. (May 11, 1959).

[12] "A Brief History of Refuge Temple." Refuge Temple is the Mother Church of the Church of the Lord Jesus Christ of the Apostolic Faith.

The school's curriculum was competitive with those of public schools that were available at the time. A 1937 edition of *The Contender for the Faith* listed study courses that included a two-year industrial course for those desirous to train themselves as workers in various trades and positions and a four-year high school training course.

There was also a regular public grammar school curriculum. These courses covered every subject that any other school carried that was considered of practical value to its students. The high school subjects included English, history, French, and instrumental music. [13]

Mrs. Carrie Sutter, an interviewee who attended the high school from 1937-1938 and taught there from 1948-1950, said Latin was taught also. According to her, several Institute students went on to outstanding high schools in New York and other cities. Those who completed the high school went on to respected colleges.

Mrs. Sutter reported that several teachers came from The Pentecostal Assemblies of the World (PAW} and the staff and teachers were black. She praised the school's facilities and remembered that they were well kept. In describing the environment at the school, she points out that,

> The school had a main building with a prayer tower on top. It also had a kitchen and dining room. The boys had a separate dormitory. There was a teachers' cottage also. The school building had several rooms, but there was a

---

[13] "Untitled Article" *The Contender for the Faith*, 1937, 5.

need to hold three or four classes in a single room. Later [in the early to mid-forties], they built an additional building with a new kitchen, a dining area, and several classrooms.[14]

Another interviewee, Mrs. Mabel Thomas, added that, in the 1950s, Lawson launched a "Buy a Brick" campaign. The raised funds were to pay for the building programs. A brick cost ten cents, and the members of the churches were encouraged to buy and sell them.[15] According to Sutter, Lawson also formed a quartet of four talented young women from the school, herself included. During school breaks and holidays, they travelled with him as far as Indianapolis and sang for various groups and churches to raise money. He also had each PAW church give a voluntary offering each month to support the Institute.

In 1939, the organization contributed $650.00 to the Institute's budget. This represented slightly more than 36% of the total disbursements of the organization and 19% of the total revenue for the COOJC annual convention.[16] This level of expenditure highlights Lawson's concern for educating young people. A 1946 convention record shows that $2,500.00 was disbursed for the R.C. Lawson Institute, a little over 17% of the $14,992.23

---

[14] Interview with Mrs. Carrie Sutter, December 28, 1989. Mrs. Sutter attended the school for a short time, completing her high school education. From there she went to Bluefield State in West Virginia for college. She returned to the institute to teach for a while. After leaving the institute, she joined the New York City school system, where she taught until her retirement.

[15] Interview with Mrs. Mabel Thomas.

[16] *Minutes of the Twentieth Annual Session*. The Church of Our Lord Jesus Christ of the Apostolic Faith, Inc. 1938-1939.

disbursed by the organization that year.[17] It is unclear whether this sizeable drop reflected increased support of tuition or other sources. However, Lawson had a genuine interest in bettering the educational experiences of inner-city youth from New York, Boston, Philadelphia, Baltimore, Trenton, and several cities in the South. Mrs. Sutter and Mrs. Thomas said the student body numbered from fifty to 150 from time to time, with the higher range being maintained around the mid- to late 1940s.[18]

Both Sutter and Thomas noted the Institute's high standards. Again, all the teachers were qualified to teach at their levels. Principals came from both the Church of Our Lord Jesus Christ and the Pentecostal Assemblies of the World. Mrs. Thomas's father, who served as principal from 1939 through 1942, had earned a BA degree from an accredited college in the South.

The school was in full operation until about the time that the Supreme Court heard *Brown v. Board of Education of Topeka, Kansas*. After the ruling that racially separate education was not equal, the Institute began to decline. Since black teachers were now able to secure better-paying public-school jobs, several left to take these positions. For example, Sutter had attended the school, and went on to Bluefield State College in West Virginia; after obtaining her degree, she returned to the R. C. Lawson Institute to teach. But after two years, she returned to the New York City school system and taught there until her retirement.

---

[17] *Minutes of the Twenty-Seventh Annual Session.* The Church of Our Lord Jesus Christ of the Apostolic Faith, Inc. 1946-1947.
[18] Interview with Mrs. Thomas.

After the Institute's closure, some of its buildings remained on the grounds as a day care facility and a residence for those who were running the program. The Church of Our Lord Jesus Christ helped support that work. The *Minute Book of the 1988-89 Annual Convention* shows that $8,956.65 was allocated for the R.C. Lawson Institute Day Care Center in Southern Pines, North Carolina. This was a small addition to the $53,763.46 that the state/federal government and tuition contributed for day care operations.

Between 1938 and 1939, Lawson opened a grocery store. The March 25, 1939, edition of the *New York Amsterdam News* pictured him testing the quality of a head of lettuce with a truck driver. The caption read, "Bishop R.C. Lawson's Organization Also Runs Grocery, Industrial Department," and the article quotes Lawson as saying,

> In practical Christian technique the approach to one in need of help, and God knows we are all in need of some form of real help, should not be with the question where one shall spend eternity, but where shall one spend the night.

The article pointed out the dramatic impact Lawson's work made in Harlem, a run-down and dangerous area of the city. It continues,

> In less than two decades, Bishop Lawson had put his socioeconomic ideas of what he called "dynamic Christianity" into practice and succeeded in carrying on

the work of the Industrial Union Institute and Training School at Southern Pines, North Carolina.

In addition to the grocery store, a day nursery was started in the building that was the 'birthplace of the Church of Our Lord Jesus Christ.'[19]

An announcement in the church's 1944 souvenir journal asks the provocative question,

DO YOU WANT YOUR CHILDREN TO BE HAPPY?

> Home Training
> Good Food
> Careful Watching
> Good Health

SEND THEM TO OUR DAY NURSERY

This was before day care centers or Head Start programs were being run and supported by the government.

Lawson's activities included civic and political dimensions, as well. The May-June 1947 issue of the *Contender for the Faith* records that he was one of two speakers invited to address a dinner at Gracie Mansion—City Hall—which would be attended by many city fathers. The account of the impact of his address recounts that he "spoke to those in authority without pulling punches" on the conditions in Harlem that might be remedied by their assistance. He implored them, "Help us clean

---

[19] "Bishop R. C. Lawson's Organization Also Runs Grocery Industrial Department." *The New York Amsterdam News,* (25 March 1939), 16.

up Harlem, give us clean streets and lots, better houses, and [fewer] rat and fire traps."[20]

His address brought a response from several city leaders. D. Levy, captain of the 32nd Precinct, followed up with a call to Lawson "to ask him how he could cooperate to bring about [a change] in the conditions" Lawson had addressed in his speech.[21]

Lawson also had a printing press in the church on West 133rd Street. He ran a bookstore that featured books on Africa and black Americans, along with religious publications and Bibles.[22]

Lawson and other local ministers were cited in an edition of a local newspaper, *People's Voice,* for taking the *New York Times, Herald Tribune*—the city's leading daily newspaper—to task for "discouraging white people from coming into Harlem" while most of the businesses in Harlem were white-owned. The article concludes,

> Bishop Robert C. Lawson in his regular Sunday night broadcast over station WBNX told his thousands of radio fans how New York dailies demanded more police for Harlem, but not once did they point out that, out of New York City's 18,200 police officers, only 132 are Negroes. Though delinquency and crime situations must be solved by the citizenry, not by the police officers, Bishop Lawson

---

[20] "Untitled Article" *The Contender for The Faith,* (May-June 1947), 5.
[21] Ibid.
[22] Interview with Mrs. Thomas.

thinks if the dailies were sincere in their desire to help Harlem, they would have demanded more black police.

The article's final paragraph summarizes how Lawson used his broadcast to deal with the city's social problems. It reads,

> The radio audience, perhaps for the first time, learned from Bishop Lawson how Harlem schools are understaffed, without sufficient textbooks and school supplies, with many teaching positions unfilled, and many holding jobs for which they had not been trained. [23]

Lawson's leadership in the fight for equality and social justice in New York City included ecumenical work with other black clergy members.[24] Among the honors this openness garnered for the Apostolic leader was Ethiopia's highest decoration: Lawson was made an honorary commander in the Ethiopian Army by Emperor Haile Selassie. He was also among those selected to read the scripture at the Prayer Pilgrimage for Freedom in Washington, D.C. on May 17, 1957, in which Martin Luther King, Jr., and other social action leaders were involved. Yet he never forgot his community. Mabel Thomas recalls during her days as his secretary, if "someone was looking for employment, all Bishop would have to do [was] give the person a note and send them downtown and they would get a job."[25]

The Discipline Books of COOLJC and Lawson's sermons attest that he was a strong Oneness preacher. Still, as Joseph

---

[23] Untiled article, *The People's Voice.* (The clipping did not carry the date).
[24] Ibid.
[25] Interview with Mrs. Thomas.

Washington would argue about Apostolics in *Black Religion: The Negro and Christianity in the United States*, his theology did not conflict with his social activism.[26] Rather, his activities were concrete expression of the faith as he understood, preached, and taught.

Bishop Smallwood E. Williams

Bishop Smallwood E. Williams founded Bible Way Church of Our Lord Jesus Christ World-Wide in 1957 and served as the denomination's Presiding Apostle until his death in 1991. During his tenure, the organization reported a membership of 500,000, with churches in the United States, Africa, England, and the Caribbean. Williams was also the founder and senior pastor of the denomination's headquarters church, Bible Way Church, in Washington, DC. He served for over sixty years with a membership of approximately 2,500. At the time of this writing, he was eighty-two years old and as his officers and staff delighted to say, was "still going strong." Along with his staff, he was supported by his wife, Verna L. Williams, and two daughters, Pearl Williams Jones and Yvonne Williams, with his son Elder Wallace Williams as assistant pastor.

People across the country, but especially those in the Washington, DC, Virginia, and Maryland areas highly respected Williams. He often gave counsel and support to such

---

[26] Joseph R. Washington, *Black Religion: The Negro and Christianity in the United States.* Lanham, MD: University Press America, University Press of America, 1984, 114-115.

notable civil rights activists as Jesse Jackson and Walter Fauntroy.[27]

In the early 1950s, the black weekly newspaper, *The Afro-American* referred to Williams as the "radio evangelist [who] might be the modern Moses that Washington is looking for to lead them out of the Jim Crow wilderness."[28]

While this is some achievement for a black Apostolic preacher, if one knew Smallwood Williams, one would not be too surprised at these achievements. From his early childhood, he seemed aware of God's will for him to be a champion for and servant to others. During our interview, he recalled that as a twelve-year-old, his mother would prepare a basket of food each Sunday morning, wrap it in a napkin, and have him take it to a blind elderly woman, Mrs. Ellis. While she ate the hot meal, he would sit and read the scriptures to comfort her "before returning home."[29]

Recalling his mother, Williams stated,

> [despite] all the children she had, and my stepfather being a laboring man... she had a heart that would go out to others. Though there were nine in the family, we were never on relief... [or] public welfare. The Lord always made a way and I never got up from the table hungry. I

[27] See, for example, Walter E. Fauntroy, "A Bicentennial Salute to Bishop Smallwood E. Williams," *Congressional Record* 121:7. (January 27, 1976), 1.

[28] Al Sweeny, "The Rambling Reporter," *The Afro-American*, (22 March 1952), 221.

[29] Smallwood E. Williams, *This is My Story. Washington, DC: Bible Way Church of Our Lord Jesus Christ, 1984.*

guess from childhood the seed was planted and having received the Holy Spirit, the Spirit of love and compassion… carried over into my ministry.

Somehow or other I constantly find myself, even at this age, being on the side of the underdog…. That's what this is all about, reaching out to people that need help.[30]

From those early days, Williams appears to have been under the guiding hand of God. He was ordained by Bishop Lawson in 1925.[31] He was something of a marvel to everyone: people began to call him the "boy preacher" because of his maturity in spiritual matters. This was the reason, no doubt, Lawson asked him to come to New York and develop his ministry under his tutelage. According to Williams, Lawson gave him the option of coming to New York with him or going to Washington, DC. After much prayer and with his mother's council that he not become a burden to Bishop Lawson, he opted for Washington. But connecting these events with the pattern of his productive life, Williams said,

These were my own inclinations. Something was born in me. Therefore, I go back to, Luke 4:18-19, that says 'The Spirit of the Lord is upon me because he has anointed me…" That's why the Lord Jesus put it on Bishop Lawson's heart to give me the choice of coming to New York or going to Washington…. It was the Lord speaking through him because it was something in me that would

---

[30] Interview with Bishop Smallwood E. Williams, February 19, 1990.
[31] Ibid.

respond to something, to what was out there on the street, and up there at the Capitol.[32]

During my interview with Williams, he elaborated on his views about his being in Washington.

> CLARK. So, is what happened with you in Washington the outgrowth of what had been at work in you from your earliest years? By voting when others in the church would not vote, you affirmed your worth as a citizen and rejected the injustices in the system as you saw them. You seem to be saying your response to these situations was not accidental.

> WILLIAMS. Right. Now you see, when I came here, Herbert Hoover was president, and there were lines of white and black folks, and the poor from all over the country were having hunger marches. The stock panic was going on. And the people were out of work all over the country, and were jumping out of buildings on Wall Street... You couldn't vote here in Washington, so I sent my absentee ballot to Columbus and voted against Hoover... because I saw the condition of the people here and everywhere.

> I was tired of poverty and deprivation. Now the churches, began to awaken. Lawson had a social consciousness. He may not have expressed it as far as I expressed it, but he was very active.

---

[32] Ibid.

CLARK. I don't think anyone has gone as far as you have in this area in our tradition.

WILLIAMS. Well, I entered it and began to be active in the early days of my ministry. When I had a lot of time, I'd go down to the Capitol to hear Senators [Theodore] Bilbo and [Huey} Long and others. I remember a senator (couldn't recall his name at the time).

There is a man that's over there now from Alabama and he went along with blacks because he…[said] if it hadn't been for them, he wouldn't be in office. Now his grandfather, I remember hearing him speak in the Congress right over there: [pointing to the Capitol] I was sitting up in the balcony when he helped pass a bill to have segregated seating in Washington on all transportation. We didn't have segregated transportation… we had it in the schools, [and there was] a general pattern of segregation in the hotels and other accommodations, but transportation was open. He said let that bill stay in there, that bill for separation of black and white. I haven't forgotten that yet. I didn't read it in a book. His grandson is over there, and I have lived to see him, and to see it turn around.[33]

This early exposure to the seat of power and the workings of government may explain why Williams, from his early ministry, preached sermons focused on contemporary social

---

[33] Interview with Bishop Williams.

issues. During this time, there was a remarkable difference between his sermons and those of his peers. Most preachers in the tradition preached mainly doctrinal sermons (i.e., messages mostly about the Godhead, Jesus is the Mighty God, and the Second Coming of Christ). While Williams also preached on these topics, he spoke on another level. He was uniquely concerned about the quality of the pilgrimage, while the believers and their fellow citizens sojourned on earth; much of his preaching reflected this concern.

We get a sense of his courage and prophetic bent in the sermon he preached while the Supreme Court justices were deciding the *Brown vs. Board of Education of Topeka, Kansas case*. While this sermon employs the Apostolic/Pentecostal hermeneutic, he also applied this stance to the sociopolitical situation of the time. The sermon entitled "The Spiritual Significance of the Supreme Court" was preached on four radio stations on Sunday, February 1, 1953. Using the "Numerical Principle," outlined he proceeded to tell his listeners the importance of the nine justices as opposed to a greater or lesser number.[34] Again, in his words,

> The number nine is the sum of the number six plus number three. For six and three are nine. The number six is man's number, and the number three is God's number. Thus, in the number nine we have the power of God working with man. Thus, we have the number nine.[35]

---

[34] Edwin Hartill, J. *Principles of Biblical Hermeneutics*. Grand Rapids, MI: Zondervan Publishing House, 1947, 109-123.

[35] Interview with Bishop Williams.

Then Williams called for the citizens of Washington to join him in praying for the nine justices, saying:

> To the American people of all races and colors, and to the honorable members of the Supreme Court, I say, "Listen to the words of King Jehoshaphat in the 19th chapter of II Chronicles and the 6th and 7th verses....

> Take heed what ye do: for ye judge not for man, but for the Lord, who is with you in the judgment. Wherefore now let the fear of the Lord be upon you; take heed and do it: for there is no iniquity with the Lord our God, nor respect of persons, nor taking of gifts.'" [36]

He closed the sermon by reiterating that prayer be offered for the justices, so that they would be mindful that justice was to be served in obedience to the will of God for "they sit as God's representatives: yes, God's agents of justice in the United States of America." [37]

It's important to point out that Williams' interest in these proceedings did not commence with the hearings but began in March 1952, when he sought to enter his youngest child Wallace into an all-white school about half a block from his home. At that time, the school board that operated under the dual system (a euphemism for a segregated system) decided to transfer Williams's son, along with several other students, from Charles Young Elementary School to the Cromwell School. This was an

---

[36] Ibid.
[37] Ibid.

inferior school compared to the Charles Young Elementary and was also segregated. Further, the Cromwell School was so far from the Williamses' residence that he or his wife would have had to walk their five-year-old son to and from school each day, which would have been a hardship for them. When faced with this prospect, Williams wrote,

> I became angry, and that is hardly a word for it. I rebelled. I refused to tolerate this social injustice any longer lying down. I decided I would stand up and be a man.[38]

A lot happens when men decide to be men or women decide to take a stand against injustice. Williams was about to buck the segregated system regarded as "the best in the country," an action he says was "a non-honor." As one might expect, his behavior was not appreciated by the Board of Education or the school superintendent. Pressure was put on the principal and teachers to thwart Williams's efforts to integrate the school. Williams fought back.

He was civil and Christian in his manner. In fact, he initiated what must be regarded as the first sit-in in the public school system in America. The headline of the *Washington Evening Star*, the newspaper with the largest circulation in Washington, DC, at the time, read "Sit-Down by Colored Minister at White School Brings Walk Out."[39]

---

[38] Williams, *This is My Story*, 97.
[39] "Sit-Down by Colored Minister at White School Brings Walk Out." *Washington Evening Star*, March 3, 1952.

Williams persisted, and the school officials resisted. Again, in his words, he told them, "I am going to stay until you let my boy go to school here."[40] Although he was defeated in his attempts and ended up enrolling his son in another school, he had not finished fighting. The *Washington Evening Star* quoted him again as saying,

> I feel most strongly that it is undemocratic, unfair, and un-American to deny my son or any other American citizen a right to attend the nearest public school to his residence, regardless of his race, color, or religion.[41]

The newspaper commended Williams for his views and his fight and questioned the wisdom of those who were advocating selective school enrollment by race or economic class.[42]

This was not the only social issue that Williams addressed. In his book *Significant Sermons*, he relates that, during the most difficult years of the Civil Rights Movement, he used his radio broadcast to rally those in the district and the surrounding areas to join in the civil rights effort and to pray for social justice. He was on four radio stations on Sunday mornings. On November 3, 1963, the Sunday morning of the bombing of the Ebenezer Baptist Church in Birmingham, Alabama, in which three young black girls were killed while attending Sunday School, he called the city's entire black population to church. In his account of the event, Williams stated that the church was packed in the main

---

[40] Ibid.
[41] Ibid.
[42] Ibid.

seating area and balcony. He began his sermon entitled "America at the Crossroads" with the passage from Amos 3:7-8, and in it declared,

> Our destination is determined not by speed, but by direction. The golden opportunity has been given to our nation to change its direction in which we have been traveling in race relations for the past century, the narrow crooked immoral road of racial segregation, color discrimination, and bias. It is a moral necessity that we change direction and get on the broad straight road of righteousness, the highway of brotherhood, love, and compassion.[43]

He encouraged those in attendance to join him in praying for divine intervention by turning to the capitol, which was less than ten minutes' walking distance away. He admonished that by doing this, they would be "making a great and profound contribution in this struggle for social justice."

He told them that the crossroads the nation faced that day was whether Congress would pass the civil rights bills that the president had submitted or let them continue to languish in committee. With the forcefulness and conviction of the prophet whose words he chose to employ, he warned,

> The time is now. I say to you, today is the day. There should be no further postponement of an end to racism in

---

[43] Smallwood E. Williams, "America at the Crossroads," *Significant Sermons,* Washington, DC: Bible Way Church of Our Lord Jesus Christ, 1970, 15.

America. That is the reason I am praying. Do you know that the Christian religion and everything that we have in morality is based on two principles? All the laws and commandments are expressed and comprehended in the words of the Lord Jesus Christ: *'Thou shalt love the Lord thy God with all thy heart,'* but He did not stop there. Had he stopped there, a lot of people would be righteous, but there is more: *'Thou shalt love thy neighbor as thyself'*[44] This should be done regardless of whether our neighbor is black or red, or rich or poor.[45]

In his sermon on Sunday, July 6, 1958, he took his text from Matthew 18:3-6, where Jesus approved of the parents who brought their little children to him. He concluded with the words,

> *But whoso shall offend one of these little ones which believe in me, it (were) was better for him that a millstone were hanged about his neck, and that he were drowned in the depth of the sea.*[46]

He titled this sermon, "A Little Rock May Become a Millstone." He used it to deal with the Little Rock, Arkansas, situation in which nine black children were being denied entrance to the city's central high school. He said,

Jesus took a little child and sat him in the midst of them and the child is still in the midst of us. Some would like to

---

[44] Matthew 22:36-40.
[45] Williams, "America at the Crossroads," 21.
[46] Matthew 18:6.

get him out of this central position—out of the spotlight—but no one would do that, because the Lord Jesus placed him in the midst of them and the child is still sitting there. Socially, morally, and judicially, the little child is still sitting in the midst of us in Little Rock, [and in] Arlington, Charlottesville, and Newport News, Virginia; Florida, Georgia, South Carolina, Mississippi, Alabama, and Louisiana.[47]

His point in this address was that the nation's failure to change its course would result in dire consequences; he warned "the 'Little Rock' will become a 'Big Rock' if the pattern set by Little Rock is followed by Virginia and other states... And if it does become a 'Big Rock' it will become a great millstone about the neck of this nation" with the result being irreversible chaos and tragedy. He concluded the message with three action items he wanted the president and Congress to take. He also appealed to his listeners to "write to the president or [their] congressman expressing similar views."[48]

Bishop Williams preached many more empowering sermons throughout the 1940s, 50s, and early 60s to thousands of members of his church and other admirers or followers. All who heard him appeared to receive strength, encouragement, and enlightenment from the words he spoke. Evidence of his influence is cited in Senator Wayne Morse's motion that one of

---

[47] Williams, "A Little Rock May Become a Millstone." *Significant Sermons,* 44.

[48] Ibid.

Williams's sermons be voted into the Congressional Record. The motion was adopted.[49]

Williams represented a growing group of Apostolics who, though holding true to the doctrinal perspective, saw Christ as triumphant and victorious over all evil. Thus, they felt that not only social, but personal, sin was to be dealt with in the name of this One who rose from the dead with "all power" and inferred in his parable in Luke 19:11-27 that those who received his resources or talents were to be engaged in activity that would gain a significant return on his investment; thus those who would follow him were to "occupy till I come."[50] The "occupational forces" or "spiritual subversives" who have been empowered by God are to serve the poor and oppressed for the kingdom of Christ. To imitate Christ effectively, Williams pointed out that,

> The black minister… has an even greater [obligation] to be politically involved… than the clergy of other races because so many unsolved problems are left over from 300 years of human slavery, exploitation… injustices and deprivations, and degradation of his people. The social sin of racism found in segregation and economic exploitation can be solved through the political process. The minister, as a man of God, must be like John the Baptist crying in the asphalt jungles in our ghettos. He has the responsibility to act politically as an individual and as a citizen to his highest level of competence and compulsion

---

[49] Ibid.
[50] Luke 19:13.

for the political principle. He must aid persons he feels will be best for his people, community, country, and even the world. The minister who is alert must think not [just] in terms of domestic policy but foreign policy as well.[51]

He viewed his role as one of making "good saints [and]... citizens" of those who followed him to achieve these objectives, he found himself engaged in just about every facet of the African American struggle in his local parish and beyond.

His commitment took him to the White House, the legislature, political conventions, and lobbyists for big business groups. He served as the district chairman of the Southern Christian Leadership Conference (SCLC) and maintained ongoing contact with authorities in major hospitals, jails, and prisons.

Further, in the early 1970s, the Bible Way Church Worldwide, under Williams' leadership, commenced a community development project in a blighted area of the city. The results of this effort had a lasting impact on the community. The church constructed two complexes in this area. The first was the Golden Rule Homes, an $8 million, ten-story residential structure with approximately 124 apartments, a daycare facility, and other amenities. The second complex was the Golden Rule Center. This was a residential and commercial complex with forty townhouses and commercial facilities. The project was "designed as a mini neighborhood with 16 of the

---

[51] Williams, "Standing on the Watchtower." *Significant Sermons*, 75.

townhouses being situated on the roof of the commercial facility. The cost for this project came to about $2.5 million."[52]

During a later interview, Williams shared his plans to build a $10 million housing complex to be called The Golden Rule Plaza, Inc.[53] In addition to one hundred units for apartments, facilities would be provided for The Golden Rule Plaza Community Cultural Center. The programs that would be provided by this Center included

> drama, music, and the theater arts, [including 'facilities and staff for teaching. There [would] be a little theater complete with [a] stage, associated dressing rooms and other facilities... [and] a complete arts and crafts studio to teach many kinds of art, sculpture, and crafts. Reading rooms and tutoring areas, [along with]... exhibition space for continual exhibits... lounge snack bars, and [areas for] passive recreation, [would] also be provided.[54]

All of this was being built in the black neighborhood of Washington, DC, and contiguous to the church's property, to meet the need for affordable housing and cultural uplift in the community. Middle-class and poorer neighbors could benefit from this major development. Again, for those leaders facing the complex situations fostered in urban centers by racism and economic exploitation, Williams offers wise and timely counsel. To those who hope to do theology that fosters social

---

[52] Interview with Bishop Williams.
[53] Ibid.
[54] Ibid.

transformation, he urges that they employ radio, television, and every available means of modern technology in their preaching and engage in street demonstrations, as well as in fasting and prayer."[55]

Bishop Lawrence G. Campbell

When you have had the privilege of listening to sermons preached by Bishop Williams Sunday after Sunday, observed him at work in the public arena on behalf of the poor and oppressed, and personally shared in the efforts to change unjust and oppressive conditions, your response to the "divine call" would take on characteristics like those of "a father in the Gospel." This was true for Bishop Lawrence G. Campbell of Danville, Virginia.

Bishop Campbell was the senior pastor of the Bible Way Church in Danville. He, along with his wife Gloria, his three sons, and his two daughters, was engaged in a flourishing ministry in this southern city. The church's membership numbers are close to six hundred and is still growing. They are presently in the process of remodeling the church, a project which, once completed, will cost approximately $1 million.

These are much happier days than the days this young Apostolic family experienced in the early 1960s. Perhaps to start at the beginning is the best way to show how the Campbells

---

[55] Ibid.

were introduced to their theological task and endeavored to fulfill it.

Campbell was born in Danville, Virginia, in 1930. He moved to Washington, DC, and was won to Christ through the ministry of Bishop Williams in 1951 when he was twenty-one years of age. In 1953, he and his wife Gloria felt the call to return to Danville to preach the Gospel.

Campbell was among the best and brightest of the talented ministers being produced by the Bible Way Church at the time, and so, much was expected of him. However, no one could have imagined the extent to which his faith in Jesus the Christ and his extraordinary talents and gifts would involve him in the history of Danville and the greatest movement for social change of this century.

According to Campbell, he went to Danville just to "preach the gospel to the lost." It was purely an "evangelistic undertaking" from which they hoped a church would grow. However, God's plan for them included evangelism and much, much more.

It all began as Campbell and his little daughter, Alethia entered the bus one day and sat behind the bus driver as they always did when they lived in Washington, DC. The driver of the bus told him, along with other vulgarities, "Nigger take your little nigger daughter and go to the back of the bus."[56]

---

[56] Interview with Bishop Lawrence Campbell, May 1989.

Campbell said all he could do was "cry as [he] struggled to get up and go to the back of the bus." Seeing him crying, his daughter Alethia started to cry, also. It was then that he vowed, "If ever the opportunity was presented for [him] to do something about segregation, [he] would do it."[57]

The opportunity came in 1961 when the black people of Danville began to resent the poor library facilities they were forced to use and decided to sit in at the library for the white citizens which, obviously, was much better equipped. This action resulted in the now famous "vertical integration" of the Danville public library. The city authorities removed all the seats in the library, making it necessary for both blacks and whites to stand. From the effort to integrate the library, the "movement," as it was being called, expanded to demonstrations at variety stores and other businesses in the city. Campbell seized this time to make his move. Using his influence as a very popular holiness preacher on the local radio station, he proceeded to advocate integration of all the public facilities. He took the city officials to task for their failure to respond to the aspirations of the black citizens to be treated equally. His efforts were met with anger by the white people of the city, and some measure of suspicion by a few of the black religious leaders of the other denominations.

According to Campbell, this was "the first time, a holiness or Apostolic preacher took this kind of action... and other church leaders and members did not know what to make of it," because

---

[57] Ibid.

they strongly supported the National Association for the Advancement of Colored People (NAACP), which was against demonstrations as a way of bringing about social change. So, Campbell and his associates eventually opted to align with the SCLC. He was not surprised that leaders of several smaller independent Pentecostal churches criticized him as well. Some went so far as to announce that Campbell had fallen out of favor with God because of his involvement in politics.

Campbell thought that though they stood to gain from the movement's success, their reaction was "a function of the theology they held" and the hardships they were experiencing because of the struggle. In the first instance, for some, a strong emphasis on the Rapture, or the Second Coming of Christ, meant they had to separate themselves from every avoidable contact with the world in anticipation of this event. Secondly, in his words, "These people had never experienced curfews before. And the brutal beatings many experienced during some demonstrations (his wife Gloria was a victim of one beating) struck such fear that many felt God was judging (him).[58]

This came to light when Campbell and two other church leaders, Baptist pastor Alexander I. Dunlap and a layperson, Julius Adams, were indicted under Virginia's John Brown Statue.

Despite these pressures, Campbell soon became one of the most respected leaders in Danville's African American community.

---

[58] Interview with Bishop Campbell.

He continued to advocate a strong activist approach to bring about needed social change. He and Dunlap were like "new wine in old wine skins"—they and their followers spurned the NAACP.[59] Aldon Morris, in his text *The Origins of The Civil Rights Movement,* shows that this was a common occurrence throughout the South as the movement began to gain momentum.[60] In the words of Len Holt,

> By impatience, because of the inspiration of nearby Greensboro, and because of disgust with the 'conservative leadership' of the Reverend Doyle Thomas of the Loyal Baptist Church of Danville and other minor reasons, the Reverend Lawrence G. Campbell, Julius Adams, and Reverend Alexander I. Dunlap activated a branch of the Southern Christian Leadership Conference in Danville.[61]

This move was met, of course, with anger by the local NAACP leadership, but the community began to refer to these men as "those boys with guts" as they set about even more vigorously to bring about change. They met frequently with the Danville City Council and demanded that,

> representation of Negroes on various boards running city agencies, school integration, desegregation of the facilities of City Hall, including the court rooms, and better

---

[59] Len Holt, *An Act of Conscience.* Boston: Beacon Press, 1965, 81-82, 11.

[60] Aldon Morris, *The Origin of the Civil Rights Movement: Black Communities Organizing for Change.* New York: The Free Press, 1984, 54.

[61] Holt, *An Act of Conscience,* 65.

recreational facilities for the Negro community along with the integration of eating facilities throughout the city.[62]

Although Reverend Lendell W. Chase, pastor of Danville's 'status' Baptist Church was made president of the local SCLC, Campbell, Dunlap, and others took more aggressive roles in attempting to bring about change. Campbell used his daily radio broadcast to keep the community aware of the nature and extent of the confrontations at City Hall.

According to Holt, in the early stages of the struggle, Reverend Chase was low-key and trusted the "City Powers" to deal honestly with them. Thus, from the beginning, because of the different perceptions of the reality with which they were dealing and the suspicions of Campbell's theological posture, the struggle was twofold, within and without.[63]

During our interview, Campbell drew on his nurturing under the leadership Bishop Williams, commenting that, "I was able to do what I had to do without feeling guilt, or fearful that I was violating the will of God." Williams's understanding and employment of Oneness theology of the name greatly influenced Campbell. For his mentor preached the name of Jesus as the name of power to carry out the divine will in this age in concrete ways and acted in concert with his preachment. Thus, Campbell's understanding of how to do God's work was shaped in the same way. It took the Danville movement to bring

---

[62] Ibid., 69.
[63] Ibid.

it out, but his message was that God was with them, so they could not lose—they had to succeed.

Campbell and his two co-activists, Dunlap and Adams, crossed the line of no return "on a hot day in August in 1962" when they signed the Danville Omnibus Integration Suit and had it filed by Len Holt in the Clerk's Office of the United States District Court for the Western District of Virginia. The white community was alarmed because this suit "asked for the integration of everything": the Danville Memorial Hospital, the Danville Technical Institute, cemeteries, the city armory, nursing home for the aged, public housing projects, all public buildings, teacher assignments, and all city employment.[64]

In addition to the Danville Omnibus Integration Suit, they pushed for more and more demonstrations seeking to engage the masses of lower income Negroes in the struggle. Their stock went "sky high" when they successfully negotiated the appearance of Dr. Martin Luther King, Jr. in Danville, where he spoke to an overflow crowd at the armory.[65] As one might expect, this success had its downside, for it was here that the most severe test of their dedication and commitment to the cause was brought to bear. Campbell, Dunlap, and several others were arrested and subsequently indicted on a felony under the 'John Brown Statute,' Section 181 1-422 of the Virginia Law, that said they had "conspired to incite the colored

---

[64] Interview with Bishop Campbell.
[65] Ibid.

population to insurrection against the white population, or the white against the colored."[66]

This move, plus an injunction against the demonstrations, was the racist community's answer to efforts of the movement leaders. The rest of the story, as presented by Len Holt, is a shocking account of the white power structure's successful efforts to break the movement's back. It demonstrates how the leaders held on, despite insurmountable odds and numerous setbacks.

The story of the "Danville Movement" shows how the Apostolic Church, led by Bishop Campbell, his wife Gloria, and other church members was fully represented in this direct confrontation with the city power. Regrettably, not enough has been written about the heroic efforts of the members of my Oneness denomination and countless others. So, to many, it appears that Oneness Pentecostals are indifferent to the issue of social justice, still preach a "pie in the sky" religion and are sitting and waiting for the Holy Spirit to do what needs to be done.

Campbell, and others transcended this tendency and stood against social injustice in his hometown. He represents a significant community within the Pentecostal/Apostolic tradition that believes there is work to be done on earth while we await the Parousia. Our Lord commands it!" To do this appropriately is to "do theology" as Frank Chikane describes it

---

[66] Ibid.

by confronting the unjust structures of society to change them, as well as reaching for those who are broken, lost, and in need of salvation.[67]

Campbell and his wife put their lives on the line for their people and stood up for what they knew to be right. In addition, they attended to those in the community who lined up before their church. This included a "Feed the Hungry" program for about 13,500 people annually. An offshoot of this effort was a "Food Bag Ministry" that monthly provided food sufficient for a full dinner for fifty families.

For several years, the church ran a camping program that sent sixty kids a week to Camp Stony Mill and a "Summer Swim" program through the YMCA & YWCA. These activities were funded by The Womack Foundation, a fund created expressly for underwriting these types of programs by a white executive of a local electronics corporation. Bishop Campbell was a member of the Board of Directors.[68]

The church's day care center had an average enrollment of forty students per month. This effort was made possible by their participation in the Title 20 program sponsored by the state of Virginia. For at least five years, they conducted a GED program that helps people to obtain a High School Equivalency

---

[67] Frank Chikane, "Doing Theology in a Situation of Conflict," in Charles Villa-Vicencio and John W. de Gruchy, eds., *Resistance and Hope: South African Essays in Honor of Beyers Naude*. Grand Rapids, MI: Wm B. Eerdmans, 1985, 98-102.
[68] Ibid.

diploma.[69] An extension Bible School program through the Virginia Seminary and College enrolled twenty-five students in a curriculum that included black History.

Further, Campbell served on the board of the Danville Community College and the Virginia Seminary and College, a Missionary Baptist organization, as well as on the board of First State Bank, one of three black-owned commercial banks in the state of Virginia.[70]

Bishop James W. Parrott and Ms. Joan S. Parrott

"My moral consciousness will not allow me to close them down."[71]

These were the words of the judge in Newark, New Jersey, who was asked to decide for the Presbyterian Church of Newark and against Pentecostal Bishop James W. Parrott, his wife Mother Ann Parrott, their family, and members of their church whom they were suing to have the Parrotts vacate their landmark $2 million church and recreation center. It was like a David and Goliath scenario, but these were two Christian groups squaring off against each other in the court of law.

It didn't start out this way. In the early 1980s, the Pentecostal preacher was asked by the white representative of the

---

[69] Ibid.
[70] Ibid.
[71] Interview with Joan Parrott.

Presbyterian Church to take over the church facility because the membership had dwindled too virtually nil.

In the words of the representatives of the church,

> We've got a building and you've got the urban ministry and what if we get together and have a merger. It would be like, a young Pentecostal Church teaching us... what if you with your urban ministry, what if you with your young people and your dynamic singing and your program, get together and we shake hands and you show us—the white people who have the money, who have the building how to deal with urban.[72]

According to Sister Joan Parrott, Bishop Parrott's only daughter, the one who gave this interview, this exchange took place sixteen years ago, in 1974. They moved into the Presbyterian property two years later, in 1976. Before talking about what went wrong, perhaps I should introduce you more appropriately to the gentle, soft-spoken pastor on whom all this furor had been heaped.

Bishop James W. Parrott, Sr., pastor of South Park Calvary-Lighthouse Temple at 1035 Broad Street in Newark, New Jersey, started a ministry along with his wife, Ann Parrott, that became a miracle of faith.[73] With only eight members and his small family, they started the church in the living room of their home on Greenwood Avenue in Newark.

---

[72] Ibid.
[73] Ibid.

After about five years of hard work and much faith, they moved to purchase a former funeral parlor and converted it into a church. Within five years of that move, their church grew so rapidly that they had to move again. They were successful in purchasing a textile warehouse that they renovated into a fine church facility.

Following this activity and carrying out the mandate he believed Christ had given him, Bishop Parrott began to preach on the street and hold street meetings. The results of these efforts were overwhelming. Joan reminisces on those days with a note of excitement in her voice:

> As a result of our family and the program in the 60s, 70s, and 80s, at one time in our church had sixty-five college-educated young people in the choir. We were all in college together.[74]

The sight of these young people standing outside this Pentecostal church intrigued Reverend Andrew Ransom of South Park Calvary United Presbyterian Church and caused him to arrange for the Lighthouse Church to take over his dying church. According to Joan, a few of the Presbyterian members remained with them for several years and then left. She believes their worship and ministry were incompatible with the tastes of those few who made it as though they would walk with these Pentecostals.

---

[74] Ibid.

This move was especially propitious for Bishop Parrott, the family, and the members of Holy Lighthouse Church. They had been engaged in social action programs for some time now, and the demands on their limited space were already out of hand. Through Joan's efforts, the church was running a GED program and an adult education program. They had a prison ministry and were engaged in feeding the homeless.[75]

The social program of the church was so effective that, according to Joan,

> Every year graduating classes from Princeton and Drew Seminaries came in for dialogue with Bishop Parrott. With Princeton, it's been about ten years and Drew just as long. This gave students a chance to see and talk about the social ministry of feeding the poor, housing the homeless, and everything in which he's involved. They could be close enough to 500 homeless and talk to them and Bishop Parrott as he talks to them.[76]

As of that time, the Lighthouse Church was feeding 560-590 people a day; there are different people each day. Although they had an interruption of services because of the dispute with the Presbyterian Diocese of Newark, they fed 68,000 homeless in 1989.[77]

---

[75] Ibid.
[76] Ibid.
[77] Ibid.

A slice from Parrott's interview is the best way to tell the exciting story of the beginnings of this outstanding ministry:

CLARK. You mentioned at one point where [your dad] would work with people within the congregation by housing them in the facility. Although you didn't state it specifically, if I recall, [you implied] that your church was always engaged in working with the community. Obviously, up to the time that he began this feeding, there was a limit [to what could be done] because, of course, of the limitation in your resources, financial resources, etc. How was the activity financed up to that time?

PARROTT. The activity was financed, mainly, by the church by raising offerings for the soup kitchen on Sundays. They started out with my grandmother [the late Mother Susan Parrott] making cornbread and soup. It started out with a group of about forty-five. Within about two weeks the number had gone to sixty. Within a month, the number had gone to ninety per day—we're talking about per day.

CLARK. So, ninety people per day were fed by your grandmother's cooking?

PARROTT. Yes, my grandmother, my aunt, and my mother.

CLARK. What prompted them [to do this] on that first day? What made them start this activity?

PARROTT. There were several people between 1980 and 1981 [and] Reagan's cuts were drastically affecting the communities, and several people...in the community [would] come to the church and say, "I'm hungry," and..."I don't have any place to stay."

My father was always going to court with somebody and one day he was in the court and he saw the two women who didn't have a place to stay—no place to stay, no place to go, and they were hungry and were talking to the judge and the judge was being very lenient and it touched my father's heart so...he said that we've got to do something about it. He went back then, as usual, and talked to the family, talked to my grandmother, and whatever project he's been in the whole family said alright, we'll do it... They got in there and started feeding those people. What grew from forty-five, sixty to ninety then started growing into 500 per day. The homeless network is tremendous. Three days a week we were at the Lighthouse Temple: Tuesday, Wednesday, and Friday. Then it went from Tuesday then Friday: they had Mondays off.

Everybody volunteered, nobody was paid—the church funded this. You know how black people who come from large families from the South know how to make meals stretch. My father, having been a procurement agent [for the United States Air Force], has always been a hoarder—we call him cheap. He would look through the papers himself, see chicken wings on sale, and go

74

out and buy 300 lbs. He would do the shopping—my aunt, mother, and all of them would do the cleaning and put the stuff together. Whatever was on sale, he would go out and get it. He did this with "spit and borrowed tape" from the church. By doing it more often, people saw [what was happening] and the word [got] around... People from white churches [even the Presbyterians]... couldn't believe it and they'd say let us help and so, they collectively as a group didn't help, it was different individuals from those churches [who] said, "My God, what you're doing is so worthwhile, here's $200." So, some churches would send $200, some churches would [collect] one offering per year and send $2,000: that would be their allotment.[78]

Joan Parrott continues this review of the feeding program's beginnings by emphasizing the fact that there was no pay for the volunteers, and Bishop Parrott's only remuneration was the satisfaction of knowing he was "feeding the hungry and clothing the naked." In her words again,

He wasn't interested in, "What's in it for me? What have you done for me lately?" And I think that's why the Lord blessed his initiative, blessed that faith that you know— taking a little, little becomes much when you place it in the hand of the Lord.[79]

---

[78] Ibid.
[79] Ibid.

Perhaps this is a good time to return to the court scene. Just before the opening quote, the judge asked the Presbyterian representatives and their lawyer, "Can you feed 500 people tomorrow?"

They answered they could not without board or committee approval. The judge postponed the hearings for thirty days to give the Parrotts and the Presbyterian Church time to work things out. But the matter was never resolved.[80] It seems that "there arose a pharaoh who knew not Joseph" in the person of a new executive director, Dr. Carol Washington. Though she also was black, the Parrotts believed she was hired as a hatchet woman for the hierarchy. But ten years of feeding the hungry, housing the homeless, and clothing the less fortunate had paid off with great results.

The Legal Aid Society, with whom the Parrotts had been working on behalf of the poor over the years, came to their rescue. The newspapers also supported them. And it wasn't long before the Parrotts discovered the real reason for their eviction: "the Presbytery" wanted to sell the property to the management of Symphony Hall. They were near bankruptcy and desperate to make a deal; no matter the cost to the poor, they stood to make a good profit from the deal.

The Parrotts lost the church, but the Presbytery lost the respect of virtually the entire city of Newark. Additionally, Joan Parrott won one of the most important fights of her life. After much

---

[80] Ibid.

prayer, and with the help of the Lord, she took on the mayor of Newark, Sharpe James.[81]

The details she disclosed in my interview with her help us to better understand the situation:

> CLARK. So…out of a ministry to the hungry and… the homeless, which is clearly, without question, a type of social action carried on by the Pentecostal/Apostolic Church… you were forced… to get involved in direct political activities…. You had to go right to the mayor [in order] to make things happen.

> PARROTT. Absolutely, and [I] had the kind of documentation of what had happened. It wasn't like, "Oh, this is what we want to do now—this is what he said to me." He threw every block in because all the preachers had been jealous of the fine reputation that Bishop Parrott and the Lighthouse Temple had for what they were doing. He said, "I have a lot of people lobbying. I have a lot of money that I'm putting out there in the community." I said, "I'm not talking about pilot programs, Mayor, I'm talking about something that has become an institution. Ask the poor who the Lighthouse Bishop is, ask them who these other people are." And there was nothing he could say to that because he knew that was a fact. It was our [long-term] involvement in social action…. It was the fact that I

---

[81] Ibid.

could just roll off statistics, social agencies, and problems and things [concerning] the homeless…that he knew to argue would have been fruitless; all he said is, "What can I do for you?"

I said to him, "Give us 487 Washington Street, and this time, you renovate it, because we've given all this time through faith and love, through spit, tape and faith, we've given it, now it's time for you."

That's when the mayor said the city can't afford to let this happen to this great institution that has been a beacon sitting on a hill.

I said to the mayor, "You have two choices—are you going to be with the greedy, or are you going to be with the needy?"

Now one of the mayor's favorite expressions is, "Yeah Bishop Parrott feeds the needy and not the greedy— he's into it; he's committed." We get calls from Atlanta, wherever the mayor is, he talks about the Parrott family, the Lighthouse community light.[82]

Joan aired a telecast-on Channel 13 with the mayor, which was very well received: there were even thoughts about making it into a documentary. The rest of the interview was filled with vignettes about the ups and downs, the joys, and sorrows of trying to meet the needs of "broken" men and women.

---

[82] Ibid.

Many lessons were learned as Bishop Parrott, Mother Parrot, Joan, and the other members of the family and church reached beyond themselves to fulfill the second greatest commandment, "Love thy neighbor as thyself." Chief among them is the need to offer even more than they had already tried to give. For, as Joan sums up,

Once the homeless come in and get saved, what do you do? We must get the schooling for them; we must get [them] grants. At this point, now, our experience has given us the information we need to write the kind of grants to get the kind of [assistance], and the Lord is just moving in all kinds of ways where that's going to be set in place.

We are truly learning how to minister with, and be in alliances with AAA, with the Holy Spirit and with drug rehabilitation. What we want to do, what I really want to do, is to go through this whole AAA thing... What's in my head is to come up with a totally comprehensive Christian program that would be the best of what we have, in addition to whatever we have learned from the homeless. So, I see that coming...and put that in manuals, put that in training manuals because we don't just want to be an institution in and of ourselves: what we should be is a teaching institution as well, because it's going to take everybody doing something.[83]

Joan talked with great emotion about the influence of her paternal grandmother on her life and spiritual development.

---

[83] Ibid.

She recalled her grandmother's speech at the denomination's national convention when she took office as the president of the missionary department: "[I] didn't know that you needed documentation to go in and take care of the sick. [I] didn't know that you needed papers or licenses to minister to a hurting family." She thought that was a scriptural initiative, Joan says. When I requested of her the kind of message she would give to her Pentecostal brothers and sisters who may not be engaged in ministry, such as the one that characterized that of her father and her family, she referenced Luke 4:18-19, and went on to say that,

> The judgment that Jesus sets up in Matthew 24 says those that have given to the poor—"I was hungry, and you fed me, I was thirsty, and you gave me drink" are the ones that get in and the ones that don't get in, the goats, are those that don't do these things....For, [of] all the things on which this judgment could be based, it's those few things. And I and our church have learned that those issues and the people that Jesus was talking about in the Matthew 25 address are at the center of where Jesus is.[84]

This ministry was the work of one Apostolic family and its small congregation in the city of Newark, a family that barely escaped the Newark riots to end up serving the needs of a deprived community with very little help from others. But with faith and single-minded devotion to the task they believed God

---

[84] Ibid.

had given them, this small band achieved what "armies" could not or would not do. And for their efforts, when the chips were down, one young female aspirant for the ministry, set upon by the Spirit of Christ, activated the top city officials to help them turn the tide for the poor. The February 28, 1989, edition of the *Newark Star Ledger* carried an article entitled "Still Cookin': James Vows New Home for Soup Kitchen." In it, the mayor is quoted regarding the 487 Washington Street site:

> It is part of the Symphony Hall redevelopment 'sleeve,' and we got proposals for housing, [and] another for an automobile business there. But there is no higher priority than this: feeding the homeless.[85]

Support from all over the city flowed in, including food-shifts and clothing. Doctors and nurses, as well as counsellors and other support staff, served on a voluntary basis.

Newspapers continued bearing the good news that the Newark church's new home would aid the poor and the homeless. The *New York Times: Metropolitan News*, July 26, 1989, carried a story and the *Newark Star Ledger*, reported that, "The Lighthouse Food Center Reopened at the New Site" with this satisfying paragraph,

> With the support of Mayor Sharpe James and the city council, a former tire factory at 487 Washington St. has

---

[85] "'Still Cookin': James Vows New Home for Soup Kitchen," *Newark Star Ledger*, (February 28, 1989).

been renovated by the city at a cost of $260,000 and leased to the center for a nominal sum.[86]

Thus, the future of the Lighthouse ministry to the homeless was bright. A groundswell of support came from other churches and various city agencies. Bishop Parrot, Mrs. Parrott, Joan, and the rest of the family sought to carry out Christ's mandate, with no thought of personal gain. They lost their lives for Christ's sake, and thus found life by serving others.

These examples do not exhaust the evidence I could present to demonstrate that Apostolic/Pentecostal churches are very much a part of the black churches that are committed to the struggle for economic and social justice in this country. Many others could be cited for a wide range of activities in this connection, including the late Bishop Winfield Showell of Baltimore, Maryland, who instituted a boys' camp in the countryside of Maryland for inner city boys in the 1950s-60s. The work of his sons and daughters, led by Franklin C. Showell, is a stellar testimony to their commitment to the social ministry.[87]

Then there is the work of Bishop Monroe Saunders of Baltimore, Maryland, and Washington, DC, who was the catalyst for the organization of two block associations in the 1960s, both of which are still active today. Bishop Saunders pastored a church of 1,000 members and growing. The church owns apartments and a single-family dwelling unit in Baltimore, as well as six

---

[86] "The Lighthouse Food Center Reopened at the New Site," *Newark Star Ledger*, (July 11, 1989).

[87] Interview with Bishop Franklin C. Showell, February 8, 1990.

acres of undeveloped land in Howard County, Maryland, which is intended for housing development.

The church recently purchased a shopping center in Baltimore and plan to convert it into a multi-purpose center to offer health, education, training, and cultural development services to the community. Additionally, they plan to convert some buildings into a library and study center for children and youth, centers for recreation, and "a family guidance center for pre-marital and marital counseling."[88]

Finally, the name of the late Bishop Charles Watkins deserves mention here. Bishop Watkins was a leader of the clergymen in Cleveland, Ohio, during the civil rights era, who invited Martin Luther King, Jr., to come to the city to launch a campaign against segregation and racism. He was also in the forefront of the move to elect Carl Stokes as the first black mayor in the United States.

What lessons have we learned from this review? Firstly, we can completely discount the received wisdom that has stereotyped Apostolic Pentecostal Churches (or all black Pentecostal churches, for that matter) as noncontributors to relieving the oppression of the poor of its constituency in their communities. Their theology fosters an aggressive response to the deprivation and suffering of the poor.

Secondly, we would have to concede, that Apostolics are perhaps no better or worse than their brothers and sisters in the

---

[88] Interview with Bishop Quick.

Baptist, Methodist, Presbyterian, and African Methodist Episcopal traditions. This fact is not meant to be a compliment, for while these traditions have been involved in social action, they have not done nearly enough or undertaken the task with any real sense of commitment. None of these traditions have engaged the problem of racism or social and economic justice as a national organization, or on ecumenical terms.

There seems to be no sense of the power an ecumenical approach to the problem would yield. These points are the subject of the closing chapters.

CHAPTER 4
An Assessment and a Strategy

Assessment

Any of the examples in the preceding chapter of Apostolics who engaged in social action could serve as a model for battling with the injustices that surround today's urban and rural centers. However, though they led national organizations, social action or social issues were not on the agenda of the national convention. When these leaders became involved with a movement or project, it naturally involved their local churches and personal resources. And while that' is commendable, this approach was only a "drop in the bucket" compared to the actual need for it committed far too little of the resources within Apostolic Pentecostalism. Racism and its related evils— economic and social injustice—are national and international problems that must be addressed on a far broader scale—not only denominationally, but ecumenically as well.

A somewhat frustrated Franklin Showell conceded that if anything significant was to be done by the churches to bring about concrete social change, it would have to be done on the local level.[1] That's the way it had been up to now. The preceding chapters demonstrate the disadvantages of not taking this approach.

Lawson, who was a pioneer in this area, at least in New York City, emerged in the era, when Pentecostal or Apostolic churches were always aiding the mostly poor members of their congregation, as well as those in the neighborhoods. The account of his childhood as the son of a Pentecostal pastor is representative of his focus on service. He told of money raised to provide food for someone who lost his job. He talked about his father's experiences with the welfare agency and how, through his personal encounters with the agency, he opened the door to assist so many others by being able to identify the best personnel to provide assistance. But he went even further.

Lawson was able to stand collegiality with other clergymen and gain from and give support to joint ventures in the metropolitan area. This possibly is why he was more progressive than his Apostolic and Pentecostal peers in the 1930s and early 1940s. When Apostolics shunned the ecumenical arena, he participated in these efforts, working with such luminaries as congressman, Rev. Adam Clayton Powell, Jr., pastor of the Abyssinian Baptist Church.[2]

---

[1] Interview with Bishop Showell.
[2] Robert L. Green, "Growing Up Black, Urban, and in the Church," *Crisis*, (November 1982), 89:9, 14-16.

His outspokenness sometimes drew considerable flak from his Apostolic brethren and other Harlem leaders, such as Father Divine.[3] Yet, though the organization that he headed was rapidly spreading along the Eastern Seaboard and in the Midwest, his social justice work was not a national project, and this involvement with social issues was not converted into a national program. Although others in the organizations preached sermons regarding the injustices of segregation, these sermons generally enjoined members to pray for change, but nothing more.

A decade later, Smallwood Williams was fighting social evil in the Washington, DC, area. Yet, they never collaborated or merged forces to aid each other in this work. On occasions when testimonials were being held for Lawson, Williams would make a tribute to and extol him for the great work he was doing. Such was the case with the Founder's Day celebration, hosted by Smallwood Williams. A 1947 issue of the *Contender for the Faith,* the national magazine for the organization, carried a report that.

> The Rev. S. E. Williams certainly gave the bishop one of the greatest receptions ever to be held in our Pentecostal movement. It [was] held in the spacious dining hall of the church and before the reception there was a play by the pastor's wife which everyone enjoyed.

---

[3] Robert Weisbrot, *Father Divine.* Boston: Beacon Press, 1984, 117.

The echo of this fine affair faded out with four ministers discussing the four sides of the bishop: The Man, The Preacher, His Achievements, and His Vision, after which there were congratulatory speeches all around, and the final presentation was made. This was a Founder's Day celebration which will long echo in the minds and hearts of the people.[4]

I have personally attended affairs where similar activities took place. Everyone was familiar with the work that Lawson was doing, praised God for him, and thanked him for his work. But no thought about broadening the effort was put forth, either by Lawson or those who followed him.

The same was true of Bishop Williams' work in Washington, DC. Lawson encouraged Williams and spoke highly of his efforts from time to time. But I found no record of any proposal by Williams to focus resources, talents, and energies on fighting social evil through the organization. Later, Bible Way Church World-Wide publications stressed the need to address drug addiction and affordable housing, but no formal program was established to deal with these matters. There was greater interest in Lawrence Campbell's efforts since by this time, the Civil Rights Movement was a national phenomenon. Still, the organization of which Campbell was a part, and over which Williams presided, did not involve itself as an organization. I was unaware of what Campbell was doing in Danville until some years later when an appeal went out for prayer for him

[4] "Untitled Article" *Contender for the Faith*, May-June 1947.

and his family because his case had come up in the courts. However, this is not to say that Bishop Williams and others were not aware of Campbell's involvement in the movement and did not make contributions to it.

There is nothing in Apostolic Pentecostal's theology that militates against real and concrete social involvement. Rather, their concept of Jesus and Jesus's authority for their lives inspires social involvement since the goal of all Apostolics is to "be like Jesus" and "do what Jesus did."

Yet, there is a perplexing reality that there is either an unwillingness or selfishness inherent in its organizational arrangements that prevents leadership from prioritizing social action issues on their national agendas. Perhaps what Gayraud Wilmore, Jr. says applies in that, "their understanding of redemption cannot admit the sanctification of secular conflict and struggle."[5] What may underlie this paradox is probably the fact that, for the most part, the activity has been reactive and not proactive. A proactive stance would involve planning and targeting areas needing attention and marshalling resources to deal with them.

An example of how detrimental and disheartening this can be was recently demonstrated in the case of the Parrott family. After ten years of faithful service to the poor, the Parrotts fell on hard times, not because they were derelict in their ministry, but

---

[5] Gayraud Wilmore, "Black Theology at the turn of the Century: Some Unmet Needs and Challenges." in Dwight Hopkins, ed., *Black Faith and Public Talk: Critical Essays on James H. Cone's Black Theology and Black Power*. Waco, TX: Baylor University Press, 2007.

because someone else had another agenda. The most logical thing to do, it would seem, would be to appeal to one's forces to aid one in the crisis.

Interestingly, while other COOLJC ministers and congregations were engaged in social action projects across the country, the Parrots did not feel they had a friend in a position of authority to whom they could turn for help. So, they struggled alone. It was only through the resourcefulness of their daughter, Joan S. Parrott, that they were able to martial the forces of the city of Newark and save the ministry. In situations like this, eventually, people begin to go it alone. And as social justice issues are starting to move into the center of focus of local churches in urban centers, national organizations stand in jeopardy of losing a great deal of local support if they do not adjust accordingly.

Strategy

Bishop Showell offered this comment during our interview:

> I think the agenda is moving toward urban ministry, [such as with] local churches like Bishop Charles Blake's church in Los Angeles [Church of God in Christ], this church in Baltimore [First Apostolic Faith Institutional Church], Bishop Smallwood E. Williams's [church] in Washington, DC, [and] Bishop Ellis's church in Detroit, Michigan [Pentecostal Assemblies of The World]. I think that's the

way [we're] going. I think the whole organizational thing is over.[6]

With his last statement, Bishop Showell suggests that the dependence on denominations for fellowship and involvement in the work of the Lord is on the wane, if not dead. The younger generation of Apostolics and other Pentecostal leaders has a different focus, it seems, and if that focus follows its logical course, then resources and talents of these local churches will be directed to these ends. Thus, there will be little, or nothing left for denominational interests that include social concerns. I pursued Showell's thinking further and share the results below.

CLARK. What will be the organizational influence in the next ten years, from your perspective?

SHOWELL. The vehicle of the next ten years will be the local churches and their urban ministry. We have geared up this area now for training our people in thirteen areas. A few are personal evangelism, media, and communications, [and] personal and family life counselling. What we do is prepare people for personal ministry in Christian service… and all is geared to community life outreach.

CLARK. So, the outreach now includes substantially more than giving out tracts and preaching on street corners.

---

[6] Interview with Bishop Showell.

SHOWELL. The only area of the thirteen areas we're working on where we do that is in the evangelistic outreach.

CLARK. But evangelism is redefined for us to include meeting the real, everyday needs of people.

SHOWELL. Whatever you encounter in the city. We have a youth ministry, a ministry to pregnant teenage mothers, we have a married couples ministry, we have a singles ministry, which addresses the needs of single people in the church. In this next decade, it's going to be single people and the elderly who are going to be the two most important ministries in the church. I see the church facility now as being the place to train people to minister in the city, a place where we come together…to praise and worship and do teaching and training for personal ministries.

CLARK. I think that's a very important concept, and I might use it as a concluding statement.

SHOWELL. What we did was, this new group of people we trained that came in our church since January 1987, they won't get locked into auxiliary groups [fundraising clubs]. We have developed a whole area of ministry. They will be on a ministry team working, for instance, for our media and outreach publications. So, the whole goal now in Christian education is training for ministry [i.e., for service to the city]. Now the ministry is redeeming the city and you tie that with the New Kingdom concept.

CLARK. What do you mean by that?

SHOWELL. I see the church as the agent in the world to prepare for the establishment of the kingdom of Jesus Christ. It's in God's plan of reconciling all things in Jesus Christ—so our concept is everybody in the church is ministering, nurturing] people inside the church...[who then] minister...to the needs of the world. So, we are preparing people to minister to the world, which is the Kingdom Concept.

CLARK. But this is in no way a subscription to the old post-millennialist perspective that the preaching of the Gospel is going to bring about the Kingdom and then Jesus will come...?

SHOWELL. It is a modern-day application of Kingdom Principles, Kingdom Living. The application of biblical Kingdom principles in everyday living today—so everybody is in as a minister of reconciliation to the world.[7]

Showell's vision represents the new trend among Apostolic and Pentecostal leaders. It is important to point out that, when he talks about mobilizing an entire church for ministry or service to the city, he is not talking about a congregation of just the

---

[7] Ibid.

poor, domestics, or laborers. This was the complexion of the Pentecostal/Apostolic Church years ago. In his congregation of close to 1,800, there are entrepreneurs, businesspersons at various levels in corporations, lawyers, doctors, and teachers who are trained from kindergarten to college-level education. Thus, Showell is talking about dedicating a sophisticated army of talented Christians to really make a significant and lasting impact on the community in many diverse areas.

Joining Bishop Showell with this perspective is another very prominent bishop whom I had the pleasure of interviewing. Bishop Norman Quick was pastor of the Child's Memorial Temple, Church of God in Christ in Harlem, and bishop of the Third Ecclesiastical District of New York. His response to my question as to whether he was unique as an advocate for the poor and the oppressed follows:

> I know countless ministers, bishops, pastors, [and] elders who share the same kind of avocation and interest in working outside and beyond the confines of the church itself on behalf of the people, taking the church [not only] as a major... spiritual organization, but as a [major] social agency to be used for the betterment of the lives of people.[8]

Here again, we have a young leader in a major Pentecostal organization who is on the cutting edge of change in his denomination. Further on in the interview, he offered several

---

[8] Interview with Bishop Quick.

examples of those leaders he knew personally who were thoroughly committed to effecting dramatic social change and who had succeeded in doing some good. Some even played a strong role in Jesse Jackson's presidential campaign. He pointed out that the new black governor of Virginia acknowledged the tremendous support Bishop Samuel Green of Newport News, Virginia, provided through his radio station. The governor was able to reach his constituency more effectively because of the wide listening audience Green's station addressed.[9]

The point is that there is a movement, and, while perhaps quiet at present, it is afoot among the present generation of leaders to move in a more direct way to bring about needed changes. Many of these leaders have been through the Civil Rights Movement and were influenced by Martin Luther King, Jr., and, to a more limited degree, Malcolm X. Many are better educated than their predecessors were. Many have even held corporate positions at one time or another, and they are bringing these experiences and skills to their ministries. What's more, there appears to be a willingness to move beyond the narrow denominational limits set by their predecessors to a more ecumenical approach.

When this change comes to fullness, one cannot tell the form it may take, but we get a hint from the words of Bishop Arthur M. Brazier of the Pentecostal Assemblies of the World who said during the mid 1960s, "The country must choose between the republic and a police state; for America cannot keep down

---

[9] Ibid.

thirty million people who are moving up, without destroying the entire nation in the process."[10]

I hear Bishop Arthur Brazier and others like him saying that their faith in Jesus the Christ and his mission calls them to a concrete and deliberate rejection of any form of oppression, a rejection that must, nonetheless, be expressed in overt, creative action. The Woodlawn Project, which he headed in the 1960s, is the best example of how this works out.

Other perspectives, too numerous to mention, are being offered by leaders across the country. I believe it's only a matter of time before there will be a coming-together under an extra-denominational banner on the order of a national conference of Pentecostal churches for the abolition of racism or social and economic injustice. I will pray and work to that end.

---

[10] Arthur Brazier, *Black Self-Determination: The Story of the Woodlawn Organization.* Grand Rapids, MI: Wm. B. Eerdmans Publishing Company, 1969.

Bibliography

"A Brief History of Refuge Temple." *Founders Day Souvenir Journal,* (August 25, 1944).

"Bishop R. C. Lawson's Organization Also Runs Grocery Industrial Department." *The Amsterdam News,* (March 25, 1939.

"Harlem's Refuge Temple Hails 38th Anniversary." *The Amsterdam News,* (May 11, 1959).

"Sit-Down by Colored Minister at White School Brings Walk Out." *The Washington Evening Star.* (March 3, 1952.).

"Still Cookin': James Vows New Home for Soup Kitchen." *The Newark Star Ledger*, (February 28, 1989).

"The Lighthouse Food Center Reopened at the New Site" *Newark Star Ledger*, (July 11, 1989).

Discipline Book, 5th ed., The Church of Our Lord Jesus Christ of the Apostolic Faith, Inc., 1983.

Chikane, Frank. "Doing Theology in a Situation of Conflict," in Charles Villa-Vicencio and John W. de Gruchy, eds., *Resistance and Hope: South African Essays in Honor of Beyers Naude.* Grand Rapids, MI: Wm B. Eerdmans, 1985.

Golder, Morris E. *History of the Pentecostal Assemblies of the World.* Indianapolis, IN: Pentecostal Assemblies of the World, 1973.

_____. *The Life and Works of Bishop Garfield Thomas Haywood (1880-1931).* Indianapolis, IN: by author, 1971.

Green, Robert L. "Growing Up Black, Urban, and in the Church." *Crisis* 89:9 (November 1982).

Hartill, J. Edwin. *Principles of Biblical Hermeneutics*. Grand Rapids, MI: Zondervan Publishing House, 1947.

Haywood, Garfield T., comp. *The Bridegroom Songs, Bethlehem Temple ed*. Detroit: The Voice in the Wilderness Publishers, n.d.

Holt, Len. *An Act of Conscience*. Boston: Beacon Press, 1965.

Lawson, Robert C. *An Open Letter to a Southern White Minister on Prejudice*, s.l.: s.n, s.d.

_____. *The Anthropology of Jesus Christ Our Kinsman*. Piqua, OH: Ohio Ministries, 1925.

Lovett, Leonard. "Black Origins of the Pentecostal Movement," in Vinson Synan, ed., *Aspects of Pentecostal Charismatic Origins*. Plainfield, NJ: Logos International, 1975, 138.

MacRobert, Iain. *The Black Roots and White Racism of Early Pentecostalism in the USA*. New York: St. Martin's Press, 1988.

McGee, Gary B. "Flower. Joseph James Roswell (1888-1970)" in Stanley M. Burgess, Gary B. McGee, and Patrick H. Alexander, eds., *Dictionary of Pentecostal and Charismatic Movements*. Grand Rapids, MI: Regency Reference Library, Zondervan Publishing House, 1988, 311-313.

Minutes of the Twentieth Annual Session. The Church of Our Lord Jesus Christ of the Apostolic Faith, Inc. 1938-1939.

Minutes of the Twenty-Seventh Annual Session. The Church of Our Lord Jesus Christ of the Apostolic Faith, Inc. 1946-1947.

Morris, Aldon D. *The Origin of the Civil Rights Movement: Black Communities Organizing for Change.* New York: The Free Press, 1984.

Reed, David A. "Oneness Pentecostalism" in Stanley M. Burgess, Gary B. McGee, and Patrick H. Alexander, eds., *Dictionary of Pentecostal and Charismatic Movements.* Grand Rapids, MI: Regency Reference Library, Zondervan Publishing House, 1988, 645-651.

_____. Pentecostal Assemblies of the World," Stanley M. Burgess, Gary B. McGee, and Patrick H. Alexander, eds., *Dictionary of Pentecostal and Charismatic Movements.* Grand Rapids, MI: Regency Reference Library, Zondervan Publishing House, 1988, 700-701.

Robeck, C. M. Jr., "Azusa Street Revival," in Stanley M. Burgess, Gary B. McGee, and Patrick H. Alexander, eds., *Dictionary of Pentecostal and Charismatic Movements.* Grand Rapids, MI: Regency Reference Library, Zondervan Publishing House, 1988, 31-36.

Synan, Vinson, ed. *Aspects of Pentecostal Charismatic Origins.* Plainfield, NJ: Logos International, 1975.

_____. "William Joseph (1870-1922)," in Stanley M. Burgess, Gary B. McGee, and Patrick H. Alexander, eds., *Dictionary of Pentecostal and Charismatic Movements.* Grand Rapids, MI: Regency Reference Library, Zondervan Publishing House, 1988, 780-781.

Thomas, Mabel and Robert C. Spellman. *The Life, Legend, and Legacy of Bishop R. C. Lawson.* Scotch Plains, NJ: By the authors, 1983.

Washington, Joseph R., Jr. *Black Religion: The Negro and Christianity in the United States.* Lanham, MD: University Press America, 1984.

Weisbrot, Robert. *Father Divine.* Boston: Beacon Press, 1984.

Williams, Smallwood Edmund. *Significant Sermons*. Washington, DC: Bible Way Church of Our Lord Jesus Christ, 1970.

_____. *This Is My Story*. Washington, DC: Bible Way Church of Our Lord Jesus Christ, 1981.

Wilmore, Gayraud. "Black Theology at the Turn of the Century: Some Unmet Needs and Challenges." in Dwight Hopkins, ed., *Black Faith and Public Talk: Critical Essays on James H. Cone's Black Theology and Black Power*. Waco, TX: Baylor University Press, 2007.

Woodward, C. Vann. *The Strange Career of Jim Crow: A Brief Account of Segregation*. New York: Oxford University Press, 1955.

Periodicals

Church of Our Lord Jesus Christ Founder's Day Souvenir Journal, August 25, 1944.

The Contender for the Faith, March 1937. Church of the Christ Publishing Co.

The Contender for the Faith, May-June 1947. The Church of Christ Publishing Co.

Index

About the Author

Eminent churchman, scholar and administrator, James I. Clark, Jr. is known to some as "Doctor," to some as "Apostle," to others as "Bishop," but to the Christ Temple of the Apostolic Faith, Inc. family, where he serves as Senior Pastor, he is "Pastor." He has served at the head of that congregation for 55 years as well as Assistant Pastor of the Greater Refuge Temple of the Apostolic Faith, Inc., from 1990-2008.

Clark also served as Presiding Apostle of the Church of Our Lord Jesus Christ of the Apostolic Faith, Inc. from 2001-2007 and 2017– 2023. He served as Apostle of then Foreign Missions in the Caribbean. He founded and currently serves as the Apostle to the Social Justice and Economic and Racial Equality Commission He is the Regional Apostle of Region IV of COOLJC.

His 30-year career in executive level in private industry includes such prestigious positions as Director of Financial Aid and Director of Minority Affairs at the Columbia University Business School, and Director of Training and Development at Pfizer Diagnostics, Inc. He also served as the third Dean of the W.L. Bonner College in Columbia, S. C. His long-standing commitment to service is exemplified in his development of special community-related programs as part of Christ Temple's mission and has found fresh expression in Pastor Clark's work in social justice. In furtherance of this part of his charge, he serves as Board Chair of Faith in New York, a member of Faith in Action, and an member of the Advisory Council to New York Mayor Bill de Blasio.

Clark holds a Doctor of Education degree from the Teachers College of Columbia University, a Master of Divinity from Union Theological Seminary, an MBA from the Columbia University Business School, a Bachelor of Theology degree from American Divinity School, and a second Doctor of Education degree in Curriculum and Instruction from the University of Phoenix.

He has been applauded through such honors as the COGME Fellowship by Columbia Business School, the National Fellowship for Black Pastors by the Congress of National Black Churches, the Bennett Fellowship by Auburn Theological Seminary, the Hudnut Preaching Award by Union Theological Seminary, The Black Achievers Award by Pfizer, Inc., and the YMCA of Harlem, New York, and the Business Service Award by Columbia Business School of Columbia University.

www.ingramcontent.com/pod-product-compliance
Lightning Source LLC
Chambersburg PA
CBHW060242030426

42335CB00014B/1569